Low Cholesterol Cookbook

A Comprehensive Guide to 200 Low-Fat, Heart-Healthy Recipes That You Can Whip Up In Minutes, Along With A 4-Week Meal Plan To Assist You in Living A Healthy Lifestyle

By

JUNE BOOTH

© Copyright 2022 **by June Booth - All rights reserved.**

This document is geared towards providing exact and reliable information regarding the chapter and issue covered. The publication is sold with the idea that the publisher is not required to render accounting, officially permitted, or otherwise, qualified services. If advice is necessary, legal, or professional, a practiced individual in the profession should be ordered.

- From a Declaration of Principles which was accepted and approved equally by a Committee of the American Bar Association and a Committee of Publishers and Associations.

In no way is it legal to reproduce, duplicate, or transmit any part of this document in either electronic means or in printed format. Recording of this publication is strictly prohibited, and any storage of this document is not allowed unless with written permission from the publisher. All rights reserved.

The information provided herein is stated to be truthful and consistent, in that any liability, in terms of inattention or otherwise, by any usage or abuse of any policies, processes, or directions contained within is the solitary and utter responsibility of the recipient reader. Under no circumstances will any legal responsibility or blame be held against the publisher for any reparation, damages, or monetary loss due to the information herein, either directly or indirectly.

Respective authors own all copyrights not held by the publisher.

The information herein is offered for informational purposes solely and is universal as so. The presentation of the information is without a contract or any type of guaranteed assurance.

The trademarks that are used are without any consent, and the publication of the trademark is without permission or backing by the trademark owner. All trademarks and brands within this book are for clarifying purposes only and are owned by the owners themselves, not affiliated with this document.

Table of Contents

Introduction	7
Chapter 1 Cholesterol and You	9
1.1 What Is Cholesterol?	9
1.2 What Is the Low-Cholesterol Diet?	10
1.3 Know Your Risk	10
1.4 Harmful Effects of High Blood Cholesterol	11
Chapter 2 Appetizers, Snacks, and Beverages	15
2.1 Chickpea-Pistachio Dip	15
2.2 Edamame Salsa	15
2.3 Chunky Salsa	16
2.4 Cranberry Fruit Dip	16
2.5 Fruit Kebabs with Honey-Yogurt Dip	16
2.6 Layered Pesto Spread	17
2.7 Mushroom Poppers	17
2.8 Mushroom Quesadillas	17
2.9 Savory Snack Mix	18
2.10 Sugar-and-Spice Snack Mix	18
2.11 Homemade Corn Tortilla Chips	19
2.12 Banana-Kiwi Smoothies	19
2.13 Purple Slurp	19
2.14 Creamy Slurp	20
Chapter 3 Soups	21
3.1 Skillet-Roasted Bell Pepper, Zucchini, and Vermicelli Soup	21
3.2 Puréed Broccoli Soup with Lemon-Infused Oil	22
3.3 Double-Tomato Soup	22
3.4 Spinach and Brown Rice Soup with Ginger	23
3.5 Mushroom-Asparagus Chowder	23
3.6 Peppery Pumpkin Soup	23
3.7 Chilled Strawberry-Cantaloupe Soup	24
3.8 Curried Shrimp Bisque	24
3.9 Thirty-Minute Minestrone	25
3.10 Rosemary-Lemon Vegetable Soup	25
3.11 Beef and Vegetable Soup with Cilantro and Lime	26
Chapter 4 Salads	27
4.1 Strawberry-Spinach Salad with Champagne Dressing	27
4.2 Mustard-Marinated Vegetable Salad	27
4.3 No-Chop Cajun Coleslaw	28
4.4 Grilled Pineapple with Zesty Blueberry Topping	28
4.5 Pasta and Sugar Snap Pea Salad	28
4.6 Fresh Herb Potato Salad	29
4.7 Mediterranean Black Bean Salad	29
4.8 Tabbouleh	30
4.9 Tuna Salad Bundles with Lemon and Dill	30
4.10 Warm Chicken and Papaya Salad	31
4.11 Melon-Chicken Salad	31
4.12 Speedy Taco Salad	32
4.13 Pork and Water Chestnut Salad with Curry Dressing	32
4.14 Layered Two-Bean Salad with Cheddar Cheese	33
Chapter 5 Seafood	35
5.1 Pasta-Crusted Fish with Marinara Sauce	35
5.2 Pecan-Coated Fillets with Corn Relish	35
5.3 Fish and Fettuccine	36
5.4 Creole Catfish	36
5.5 Crunchy Fish Nuggets with Lemon Tartar Sauce	37
5.6 Broiled Halibut with Chunky Tomato-Cream Sauce	37
5.7 Halibut with Green Tea Glaze	38
5.8 Grilled Salmon with Mango-Lime Cream Sauce	39
5.9 Jerked Salmon with Raspberry-Mint Salsa	39

5.10 Spinach-Topped Salmon 39
5.11 Salmon and Brown Rice Bake 40
5.12 Spicy Sole and Tomatoes 40
5.13 Baked Tilapia with Pineapple Reduction 41
5.14 Tex-Mex Tilapia Packets 41
5.15 Broiled Tilapia with Black Bean Salsa 42
5.16 Grilled Trout with Creamy Caper-Dill Sauce 43
5.17 Smoky Trout with Citrus Topping 43
5.18 Spice-Baked Trout Fillets 43
5.19 Tuna with Ginger Bok Choy 44
5.20 Pan-Seared Tuna with Mandarin Orange Pico de Gallo 44
5.21 Tuna-Noodle Casserole 45
5.22 Tuna-Topped Barley with Kalamata-Basil Tomatoes 45
5.23 Dilled Albacore Cakes 46
5.24 Mussels in Creamy Wine Sauce 46
5.25 Lemon-Garlic Scallops 47
5.26 Sherried Seafood Sauté 47
5.27 Speedy Shrimp and Pasta 48

Chapter 6 Poultry 49
6.1 Marinated Hoisin Chicken 49
6.2 Baked Chicken with Winter Vegetables 49
6.3 Chicken-and-Clementine Kebabs with Peach Glaze 50
6.4 Baked Chicken with Crunchy Basil-Parmesan Pesto 50
6.5 Chinese-Style Chicken 51
6.6 Grilled Chicken with Strawberry-Fig Sauce 51
6.7 Skillet Chicken with Dried Berries 52
6.8 Chicken with Fresh Fruit and Veggie Salsa 52
6.9 Lemony Chicken with Tarragon Oil 53
6.10 Cheesy Oven-Fried Chicken 53
6.11 Chicken with Leeks and Tomatoes 54
6.12 Lemon-Pepper Chicken over Pasta 54
6.13 Coriander-Coated Chicken 55
6.14 Spicy Peanut Chicken 55
6.15 Barbecue-Simmered Chicken Chunks 56
6.16 Baked Dijon Chicken 56
6.17 Poultry and Mango Stir-Fry 56
6.18 Lemon-Sauced Chicken with Asparagus 57
6.19 Light Chicken Chili 57
6.20 Chicken and Rice with Herbs 58
6.21 Plum Good Chicken 58
6.22 Quick Cassoulet 59
6.23 Chicken Jambalaya 59
6.24 Chicken Tenders in Creamy Herb Sauce 60
6.25 Chicken with Broccoli and Bulgur 60
6.26 Chicken and Black Bean Tacos 61
6.27 Grilled Chicken Burgers 61
6.28 Cornmeal Chicken Muffinwiches 62
6.29 Turkey Tenderloin with Cranberry-Jalapeño Sauce 62
6.30 Southwestern Turkey Stew 63
6.31 Roast Turkey Tenderloin with Mashed Sweet Potatoes and Fruit 63
6.32 Turkey Medallions with Rosemary-Mushroom Gravy 64
6.33 Turkey and Artichoke Fettuccine 64
6.34 Velvet Turkey and Herbs 65
6.35 Currant Turkey with Capers 65
6.36 Fresh Herb Turkey Loaf 66

Chapter 7 Meats 67
7.1 Molasses-Marinated Tenderloin 67
7.2 Beef Tenderloin on Herbed White Beans 67
7.3 Flank Steak with Blueberry-Pomegranate Sauce 68
7.4 Pepper-Rubbed Beef with Mushroom Sauce 69
7.5 Grilled Sirloin Steak with Lemony Horseradish

Sauce 69

7.6 Ginger Beef and Broccoli Stir-Fry 70

7.7 Sliced Sirloin with Leek Sauce 70

7.8 Steak with Sun-Dried Tomatoes 71

7.9 Sirloin with Orange-Coriander Glaze 71

7.10 Beef Fajitas in Lettuce Wraps 72

7.11 Moroccan Beef and Barley 72

7.12 Easy Oven Beef Stew 73

7.13 Quick-Fix Chicken-Fried Steak 73

7.14 Espresso Minute Steaks 74

7.15 Cajun Meat Loaf 75

7.16 Healthy Joes with Pasta 75

7.17 Southwest Shepherd's Pie 76

7.18 Pork Roast with Horseradish and Herbs 76

7.19 Pork and Rhubarb Bake 76

7.20 Hearty Pork and Onion Stew 77

7.21 Three-Pepper Pork 78

7.22 Sesame Pork Tenderloin 78

7.23 Pesto Pork Pinwheels 78

7.24 Pork Medallions with Sautéed Mushrooms 79

7.25 Maple-Bourbon Pork Medallions 79

7.26 Pork Chops with Honey-Lemon Sauce 80

7.27 Tropical Pork Chops 80

7.28 Pork Chop and Sweet Potato Skillet 81

7.29 Double-Apricot and Ham Kebabs 81

7.30 Rosemary Lamb Chops with Lemon Sauce 81

7.31 Curried Lamb Stroganoff 82

7.32 Kiwi Veal 82

7.33 Veal Scaloppine in Shiitake Cream Sauce 83

Chapter 8 Vegetarian Entrées 85

8.1 Spicy Penne with Greens and Beans 85

8.2 Rotini with Creamy Basil-Edamame Sauce 85

8.3 Tangy Yogurt-Tomato Fusilli 86

8.4 Mediterranean Penne with Pine Nut Tomato Sauce and Feta 86

8.5 Peanut Pasta and Vegetables 87

8.6 Creamy Green Rice and Black Beans 88

8.7 Three-Bean Chili 88

8.8 White-Bean Veggie Burgers with Avocado Topping 89

8.9 Meatless Tamale Pie 89

8.10 Double-Bean Lettuce Wraps 90

8.11 Vegetarian Couscous Paella 90

8.12 Lentils with Green Beans, Carrots, and Dried Currants 91

8.13 Barley and Veggie Stew with Mozzarella and Parmesan 91

8.14 Quinoa-Vegetable Patties 92

8.15 Chickpeas and Quinoa with Mango Chutney 92

8.16 No-Yolk Egg Salad Pita Sandwiches 93

8.17 Cheddar and Vegetable Crustless Quiche 93

8.18 Greek Omelet 94

8.19 Green Chile and Tortilla Casserole 94

8.20 Lettuce Bundles with Sweet Lime Soy Sauce 95

8.21 Mushroom Goulash 95

8.22 Apricot-Teriyaki Tofu Stir-Fry 96

8.23 Tofu Parmesan 96

8.24 Sesame Tofu and Vegetable Stir-Fry 97

8.25 Tempeh with Asian Slaw 98

8.26 Summer Succotash with Creamy Polenta 98

8.27 Bean-Filled Chiles Rellenos 99

Chapter 9 Vegetables and Side Dishes 101

9.1 Roasted Asparagus and Mushrooms with Rosemary 101

9.2 Toasted Barley Pilaf 101

9.3 Broccoli with Creamy Dijon Sauce 102

9.4 Red Potatoes with Creamy Dijon Sauce 102

9.5 Brussels Sprouts with Orange-Sesame Sauce 102

9.6 Gingered Bulgur and Dried Apricots 103

9.7 Cauliflower with Peanut Dipping Sauce 103

9.8 Colorful Lemon Couscous 103

9.9 Green Bean Toss-Up 104

9.10 Citrus Kale with Dried Cranberries 104

9.11 German-Style Noodles 105

9.12 Bow Tie Pasta with Spinach and Radicchio 105

9.13 Angel Hair Pasta with Red Pepper and Tomato Sauce 105

9.14 Sesame Pasta and Vegetables 106

9.15 Sugar-Kissed Snow Peas and Carrots 106

9.16 Fresh Herb Polenta 107

9.17 Crisp Skin-On Oven Fries 107

9.18 Garlic Quinoa 107

9.19 Brown Rice Pilaf with Mushrooms 108

9.20 Southwestern Rice 108

Chapter 10 Bread and Breakfast dishes 109

10.1 Easy Mexican Cornbread 109

10.2 Garden Herb Biscuits 109

10.3 Bran Muffin Breakfast Trifle 110

10.4 Refrigerator Bran Muffins 110

10.5 Apple-Spice Coffee Cake with Walnuts 111

10.6 Confetti Scrambler 112

10.7 Rise-and-Shine Cookies 112

10.8 Whole-Wheat Buttermilk Pancakes with Blueberry-Maple Syrup 112

10.9 Homemade Muesli 113

10.10 Overnight Mixed-Grain Cereal 113

10.11 Mandarin Breakfast Parfaits 114

Chapter 11 Desserts 115

11.1 Easy Cherry-Cinnamon Crisp 115

11.2 Chocolate-Banana Mini Cupcakes 115

11.3 Cranberry-Studded Rice Pudding with Sweet Orange Sauce 116

11.4 Balsamic Berries Brulé 117

11.5 Grilled Peaches with Almond Liqueur 117

11.6 Minty Fruit Parfaits 118

11.7 Sherbet Parfaits 118

11.8 Ice Cream with Fresh Strawberry Sauce 118

11.9 Dried-Fruit Truffles 119

Chapter 12 4 Week Meal Plan 121

Conclusion 125

Introduction

No matter how busy life gets, one constant remains: We all need to eat. Over the past few decades, however, the ways we meet that basic need has changed dramatically. With today's hectic lifestyles, it's tempting to opt-out of cooking altogether, especially now that fast food is available on almost every corner. Yet taking a convenient shortcut instead of preparing meals at home can also shortchange your health. If you're looking for a better alternative to takeout and convenience foods, cooking healthy meals at home is the smartest way to go—and putting those healthy meals on the table doesn't have to take any more time than you're spending now to get processed foods.

Many people agree that maintaining the right amounts of cholesterol can be key to heart health, but if you are unsure what to eat to keep your cholesterol in balance or are even confused about what cholesterol is, you are not alone. Although much maligned, this waxy substance is needed—in the right proportion—to create hormones and vitamins as well as to help you digest food. And it keeps your cells and nerves healthy and intact.

Even when cholesterol collects in your arteries, research now shows that it is there to cover and compensate for damage that can sometimes occur to your artery walls. Problems may arise, however, when too much cholesterol collects in the bloodstream and obstructs passageways that lead to your heart and brain. While nobody would intentionally sabot their blood vessel, it's thinkable to do just that with the food selections that they make. Ordering fast food on a time-crunched schedule, grabbing a sweet treat to boost energy, or equating comfort food with only fat-laden meat-and-potatoes meals are behaviors that can raise unhealthful cholesterol levels. If you think that more people die from a broken heart than any other ailment, you are essentially correct.

Heart disease is the leading cause of death in most countries across the globe, over the age forty-five, and high cholesterol is one of the known risk factors. One in six adults, or 17 percent of the U.S. population, has high cholesterol. According to the Centers for Disease Control and Prevention (CDC), people with high cholesterol have twice the risk of heart disease as people with normal levels.

While these numbers can be alarming, if you have been told that you need to lower your cholesterol—or if you're trying to eat healthier—this book will help you take a few basic steps to achieve or maintain low cholesterol and keep it at a healthful level for life. It will also answer your questions about this complex and often baffling substance in practical, easy-to-understand terms. You'll feel confident to tackle cholesterol-related health issues head-on, especially once you discover the tempting array of tasty cholesterol-lowering appetizers, side dishes, entrées, and desserts.

Chapter 1 Cholesterol and You

Eating well is one of the joys of life. Because you want foods that both taste good and promote good health, this cookbook offers you lots of excellent choices ranging from appetizers to desserts, all high in flavor but low in saturated fat, trans fat, and cholesterol. These three substances—especially saturated fat—are the dietary villains that cause your blood levels of harmful low-density lipoprotein cholesterol (LDL, the "bad" cholesterol) to rise. That's a serious concern because high cholesterol is a major risk factor for heart disease. The more LDL cholesterol circulating in your blood, the greater your risk.

You can take three important steps to help manage your risk of heart disease. First, assess your situation and identify all your risk factors. Second, start reducing your LDL cholesterol level—and other risk factors—by making smart decisions about your diet and lifestyle. Third, commit to making good choices for the long term to live a longer, healthier life.

1.1 What Is Cholesterol?

Cholesterol is a waxy, fat-like substance found in your body and many foods. While the media may have bombarded you with the belief that all cholesterol is bad, the opposite is true. Your body requires cholesterol for many important functions: It is vital in making hormones like testosterone, estrogen, and progesterone; it makes digestive acids (commonly called bile), and it is used in the myelin sheath covering your nerves. You get approximately 90 percent of the body's daily cholesterol requirement from your liver, and 10 percent is obtained from the diet.

The liver makes cholesterol, and the intestines absorb cholesterol from food and digestive acids. For some people, the liver produces more cholesterol than the intestines can absorb. Others end up with too much cholesterol because of lifestyle factors, including the foods they eat, the amount of activity they get, and the rate at which their bodies break down cholesterol. A healthful diet and regular exercise can help balance your cholesterol levels and improve your cardiovascular system, which includes the heart and blood vessels that carry nutrients and oxygen to the rest of your body.

High-density lipoprotein cholesterol (HLD)
Known as "good" cholesterol, HDL, or high-density lipoprotein removes LDL cholesterol from the circulation and transports it to the liver, processed and expelled as bile salts. Helps eliminate LDL cholesterol and reduces atherosclerosis and plaque development with this kind of cholesterol. Your HDL cholesterol levels should be over 40 mg/dL for a healthy body. HDL cholesterol levels may be significantly influenced by making smart dietary and activity choices.

Low-Density Lipoprotein Cholesterol (LLD)
Known as "bad" cholesterol, LDL, or low-density lipoprotein, it is responsible for

transporting cholesterol from the liver to the body's cells. Plaque, which may build up on artery walls and clog the arteries, may be made up of LDL cholesterol, according to studies. Ideally, your LDL cholesterol should be under 100 milligrams per deciliter of blood. Higher than 160 mg/dL is considered excessive.' Changes in diet and exercise may have a positive effect on the levels of this kind of cholesterol.

1.2 What Is the Low-Cholesterol Diet?

If your cholesterol numbers are too high—or too low—it can seem like an arduous task to nudge those numbers in the right direction. Although cholesterol is vital for your body to function, the key is balance—having just the right amounts of both low-density lipoprotein (LDL) and high-density lipoprotein (HDL) cholesterol. Current National Cholesterol Education Program guidelines say your body's total cholesterol should be no more than 200 mg/dL (mg per deciliter of blood), which breaks down to 100 mg/dL or less LDL (often termed "bad" cholesterol) and 40 mg/dL or higher HDL ("good" cholesterol).

Although a default method for lowering bad cholesterol is using a medication, research shows that certain nutrients in foods, when working in combination, can be as powerful as medicine. While taking a little longer, natural methods help lower heart disease and stroke risk without some of the negative side effects associated with medications. If you are already taking a cholesterol-lowering medication, the dietary changes recommended here can enhance its effectiveness.

1.3 Know Your Risk

The first step is to assess your risk for heart disease. Risk factors are the behaviors and conditions that increase your chance of developing a disease. Some risk factors—aging and the medical history of your family—can't be changed. Fortunately, most risk factors can be changed. Lifestyle choices such as smoking and physical inactivity, as well as conditions such as high blood cholesterol, high blood pressure, overweight and obesity, and diabetes, are all factors that you can do something about. Heart disease is largely preventable. Before you can make changes, though, you need to identify the risk factors you can personally control. For example, your levels of total cholesterol, LDL cholesterol, and high-density lipoprotein cholesterol (HDL, the "good" cholesterol)—determined with a simple blood test—help identify your risk of heart disease. (Refer to Appendix D for a detailed explanation of how cholesterol affects your heart health.) If you don't know your numbers for blood cholesterol, blood pressure, and blood glucose, visit your healthcare provider and find out what they are.

When your numbers are available, go through this Risk Assessment checklist. The more factors you check, the higher your risk of heart disease. (For more information, see Appendix E.) For a complete personalized risk assessment, talk with your healthcare provider. Risk factors triggering heart disease are of two types.

Risk factors you cannot change:
- Age, if you're a man over 45 years or if you're a woman over 55 years
- Family history of premature heart disease

Risk factors you can change:
- Weight if you are overweight or obese (see the BMI chart on this page)
- A waist measurement of 35 inches or more for a woman or 40 inches or more for a man
- Total cholesterol of 240 mg/dL or more (see the chart on this page)
- LDL ("bad") cholesterol of 100 mg/dL or more
- HDL ("good") cholesterol less than 40 mg/dL for a man or less than 50 mg/dL for a woman
- Blood pressure of 130/85 mm Hg or more
- Triglyceride level of 150 mg/dL or more
- A blood glucose level of 100 mg/dL or more
- Less than 30 minutes of physical activity on most days
- Smoking or exposure to secondhand smoke

1.4 Harmful Effects of High Blood Cholesterol

The circulatory and cardiovascular systems. Having a high level of LDL cholesterol puts you at risk of clogging your arteries and reducing your flexibility. Atherosclerosis is a condition in which the arteries harden. Your heart needs to work harder to pump blood through tight arteries, which reduces blood flow. The buildup of plaque in your arteries may lead to heart disease over time.

The endocrine system

The hormone-producing glands in your body need cholesterol to generate estrogen, testosterone, and cortisol, among other hormones. The levels of cholesterol in your body may also be influenced by hormones. HDL cholesterol levels increase throughout a woman's menstrual cycle, while LDL cholesterol levels fall, according to studies. Menopause, when estrogen levels decline, may raise a woman's risk of heart disease in part because of this.

Increases in total and LDL cholesterol are caused by hypothyroidism, a condition in which thyroid hormone synthesis is reduced. It is the opposite consequence that occurs when there is an excess of thyroid hormone (hyperthyroidism). As a result of androgen deprivation treatment, LDL cholesterol levels may rise. LDL cholesterol levels might also rise due to a growth hormone deficit.

The nervous system

The human brain cannot function without cholesterol. About a quarter of the body's total cholesterol supply is found in the brain. The brain's ability to interact with the rest of the body is made possible by this fat, which is required for the growth and protection of nerve cells. Cholesterol is necessary for brain health, but too much of it may be harmful. Having too much cholesterol in the arteries may cause strokes, which can cause memory loss, mobility problems, trouble eating and speaking, and other symptoms. Memory and mental function loss have been linked to high blood cholesterol on their own. Beta-amyloid plaques, the sticky protein deposits that harm the brain in persons with Alzheimer's disease, may develop faster in those with high blood cholesterol levels.

Gastrointestinal/Digestive System

Cholesterol is required to generate bile, which aids digestion and absorption of nutrients in the small intestine. Your gallbladder becomes filled with crystals and hard stones if your bile contains too much cholesterol. Pain from gallstones is not uncommon.

When Cholesterol Is Too High?

Cholesterol and triglyceride levels are just a part of the coronary heart disease (CHD) equation. Other important factors can be controlled with diet and exercise. The way cholesterol behaves in your body is affected by several factors.

Inflammation

Some researchers believe that heart disease is an inflammatory disease. That means that the walls of arteries and veins are irritated or inflamed by free radicals and other compounds like cigarette smoke and food preservatives and additives. Your doctor can gauge inflammation by measuring C-reactive protein (CRP) in the blood. High CRP levels along with high cholesterol indicate a dramatically increased risk of heart disease. When LDL cholesterol is transported to the arteries, it may be acting as a steroid, trying to help reduce the inflammation. So having a high LDL cholesterol level may indicate inflammation in your arteries. Eating foods that help reduce inflammation may be one way to help prevent the risk of heart disease. Foods that contain antioxidant phytochemicals and are high in fiber can help reduce inflammation in your body.

Plaque

Inflammation can lead to the formation of plaque in the artery walls. Plaque is a combination of fats, cholesterol, and components that clot blood. Over time, hardened (or healed) plaque can build up and restrict or even stop blood flow; this is what causes 30 percent of heart attacks. Scientists have discovered that many heart attacks are caused by soft or vulnerable plaque. Other factors like high blood pressure can make the plaque covering burst or crack, causing an injury to the artery wall. The body responds by forming a blood clot, which can break free and cause a heart attack. Soft plaque is filled with LDL cholesterol. Reducing LDL cholesterol, eating for good health, engaging in moderate exercise, and taking prescription drugs can all help slow plaque formation.

Oxidation

Research shows that cholesterol that has oxidized becomes much more dangerous. Oxidation occurs when free radicals, which are unstable molecules missing an electron, take an electron from a cholesterol molecule, creating oxysterols. These then attack blood vessels, promoting lesions and fatty streaks. To fight this, consume foods high in antioxidants. These compounds, including beta-carotene and vitamin E, react or bind with the free radicals, stopping the oxidation reaction in its tracks.

Chapter 2 Appetizers, Snacks, and Beverages

It is the primary job of appetizersto boost your appetite and ready you for the subsequent main dish. The tastes of appetizersare often synchronized with the flavorsof the main course in a dinner since appetizersare the first item that we eat gives us a sense of what will be served for the main course later in the evening. An appetizeris intended to pique your interest and make you hungrier for the following main coursethat follows. This is where the term "appetizer" originates from, which translates as "something to stimulate the appetite" or "anything to appetize" in English.

It is expected thatappetizers will be served before and in additionto a meal. Thus, even if the appetizerhas a 45 percent increase in food costs, the appetizeris still gaining in revenues for the restaurant. If you can maintain your rates cheaply while maintaining the high quality of your completed product, you will be much better off. Rather thanbeing large in size and cost, appetizersshould be little in flavorand cost. The appetizershould have a unique, spicy flavorand as well as appetite-stimulating properties. When it comes to the production of pickled and salty foods, acids, pepper, and paprika all play an important role.

2.1 Chickpea-Pistachio Dip

Servings: 7 persons

Preparation time: 8 minutes

Cooking time: 3 to 4 minutes

Nutritional information: (Per Serving) Calories 106, Total Fat 2.5 g, Carbohydrates 16 g, Protein 5 g

Ingredients:

- ½ cup fat-free sour cream
- 2 medium green onions, chopped
- 3 tablespoons shelled pistachios, dry-roasted
- 2 tablespoons snipped fresh dillweed
- 1 tablespoon fresh lemon juice
- 1 tablespoon plain rice vinegar
- 1 teaspoon bottled minced garlic or 2 medium garlic cloves, minced
- ½ teaspoon olive oil (extra-virgin preferred)
- ½ teaspoon red hot-pepper sauce
- 1/8 teaspoon salt

Directions:

- In a food processor or blender, process all the ingredients for 20 seconds or until almost smooth. Serve or refrigerate in an airtight container for up to two days

2.2 Edamame Salsa

Servings: 8 persons

Preparation time: 10 minutes

Cooking Time: 0 minutes

Nutritional information: (Per Serving): Calories 37, Total Fat 2.0 g, Carbohydrates 3 g, Protein 2 g

Ingredients:

- ¾ cup frozen shelled edamame, thawed and patted dry
- 1 medium tomato, diced
- ½ medium cucumber, peeled and diced
- ½ to 1 medium fresh jalapeño, seeds and ribs discarded, finely chopped
- ¼ cup finely chopped red onion
- 2 tablespoons snipped fresh mint
- 2 teaspoons grated lemon zest
- 2 tablespoons fresh lemon juice
- 2 teaspoons olive oil (extra-virgin preferred)
- 1/8 teaspoon salt

Directions:

- In a bowl, gently stir together all the ingredients. Serve immediately for peak flavor.

2.3 Chunky Salsa

Servings: 8 persons
Preparation time: 7 minutes
Cooking Time: 0 minutes
Nutritional information: (Per Serving): Calories 16, Total Fat 0.0 g, Carbohydrates 3 g, Protein 1 g
Ingredients:

- ½ medium green or yellow bell pepper, chopped
- 2 medium green onions, sliced
- 2 tablespoons snipped fresh cilantro or parsley
- 1 tablespoon white wine vinegar
- ½ teaspoon ground cumin
- ½ teaspoon bottled minced garlic or 1 medium garlic clove, minced
- 1/8 teaspoon red hot-pepper sauce

Directions:

- In a bowl, stir together all the ingredients. Serve or refrigerate in an airtight container for up to one week.

2.4 Cranberry Fruit Dip

Servings: 4 persons
Preparation time: 5 minutes
Cooking Time: 0 minutes
Nutritional information: (Per Serving): Calories 79, Total Fat 0.0 g, Carbohydrates 19 g, Protein 2 g
Ingredients:

- ½ cup fat-free vanilla, lemon, or peach yogurt
- ½ cup whole-berry cranberry sauce
- ¼ teaspoon ground cinnamon
- 1/8 teaspoon ground ginger

Directions:

- In a bowl, stir together all the ingredients. Serve or refrigerate in an airtight container for up to three days.

2.5 Fruit Kebabs with Honey-Yogurt Dip

Servings: 4 persons
Preparation time: 5 minutes
Cooking Time: 0 minutes
Nutritional information: (Per Serving): Calories 107, Total Fat 0.5 g, Carbohydrates 25 g, Protein 3 g
Ingredients:

- ½ cup fat-free plain yogurt
- 1 tablespoon honey
- 1 teaspoon poppy seeds
- ½ teaspoon of vanilla extract
- ¼ teaspoon ground ginger
- 1 medium green kiwifruit, peeled and halved lengthwise, each half cut into 4 wedges
- 12 pineapple chunks, fresh or canned in their juice, drained if canned
- 1 small banana, cut into 12 slices
- 12 red or green grapes, or a combination

Directions:

- In a small bowl, whisk the dip ingredients. Put aside.
- Using four 10-inch wooden skewers, thread in any order 2 kiwifruit wedges, 3 pineapple chunks, 3 banana slices, and 3 grapes on each. Serve the kebabs with the dip.

2.6 Layered Pesto Spread

Servings: 4 persons

Preparation time: 8 to 10 minutes

Cooking Time: 0 minutes

Nutritional information: (Per Serving): Calories 51, Total Fat 2.5 g, Carbohydrates 3 g, Protein 5 g

Ingredients:

- 1 cup fat-free cottage cheese
- 2 tablespoons Crunchy Basil-Parmesan Pesto or commercial pesto
- Paprika (optional)
- Several fresh basil leaves (optional)

Directions:

- Put the cottage cheese in a sieve. Drain well, using the back of a large spoon to press out as much liquid as possible. Transfer the cottage cheese to a food processor or blender. Process until smooth (there should be about ¾ cup).
- Line a 1-cup custard cup or mold with plastic wrap. Spread ¼ cup cottage cheese over the bottom. Spread 1 tablespoon pesto over the cottage cheese. Repeat the layers, ending with the cottage cheese. Cover and refrigerate for 2 to 8 hours before serving.
- At serving time, uncover the custard cup and invert the spread onto a serving plate. Remove the cup and carefully peel off the plastic wrap. Sprinkle the spread with paprika. Garnish with basil.
- Chill for 8-10 hours.

2.7 Mushroom Poppers

Servings: 8 persons

Preparation time: 12 to 15 minutes

Cooking time: 8 to 10 minutes

Nutritional information: (Per Serving): Calories 44, Total Fat 1.0 g, Carbohydrates 6 g, Protein 4 g

Ingredients:

- 2 large egg whites
- 2 teaspoons water
- ⅔ cup plain panko (Japanese breadcrumbs)
- ¼ cup shredded or grated Parmesan cheese
- 1 teaspoon dried Italian seasoning, crumbled
- ½ teaspoon dried basil, crumbled
- ¼ teaspoon pepper
- 1 pound bite-size whole button mushrooms (about 32

Directions:

- Heat the oven to 450°F.
- In a small shallow dish, whisk together the egg whites and water.
- In a large shallow dish, stir together the remaining ingredients except for the mushrooms.
- Put the dishes and a large baking sheet in a row in, an assembly-line fashion. Dip several mushrooms in the egg white mixture, turning to coat and letting any excess drip off. Dip in the panko mixture, turning to coat and gently shaking off any excess. Transfer to the baking sheet. Repeat with the remaining mushrooms, arranging them in a single layer on the baking sheet.
- Bake for 8 to 10 minutes, or till the coating is lightly browned

2.8 Mushroom Quesadillas

Servings: 6 persons

Preparation time: 6 to 8 minutes

Cooking Time: 10 to 12 hours

Nutritional information: (Per Serving): Calories 100, Total Fat 2.5 g, Carbohydrates 15 g, Protein 5 g

Ingredients:

- Cooking spray
- 8 ounces of pre-sliced button mushrooms (about 2½ cups)
- ½ medium onion, thinly sliced and separated into rings
- 1 teaspoon of bottled minced garlic or 2 medium garlic cloves, minced
- 3 tablespoons of snipped fresh cilantro
- 3 8-inch of fat-free whole-wheat flour tortillas (lowest sodium available)
- ¼ cup plus 2 tablespoons shredded low-fat Monterey Jack cheese with jalapeño or low-fat Cheddar cheese

Directions:

- Heat the oven to 350°F.
- Lightly spray a large skillet with cooking oil spray. Cook the mushrooms, onion, and garlic over medium heat for 5 to 7 minutes, or till the onion is soft, stirring occasionally. Stir in the cilantro. Remove from the heat.
- Spread the mushroom mixture on half of each tortilla. Sprinkle the Monterey Jack over the mushroom mixture. Fold the plain half of each tortilla over the filling. Transfer to a baking sheet.
- Bake for 5 minutes, or till the filling is hot and the cheese has melted. Cut each quesadilla into 4 wedges. Serve warm

2.9 Savory Snack Mix

Servings: 10 persons

Preparation time: 5 minutes

Cooking time: 25 minutes

Nutritional information: (Per Serving): Calories 73, Total Fat 3.0 g, Carbohydrates 9 g, Protein 2 g

Ingredients:

- 6 4-inch rice or popcorn cakes, broken into bite-size pieces
- 2 cups bite-size low-sodium cheese-flavored or plain crackers (any shape)
- 2 tablespoons light tub margarine,
- ½ teaspoon chili powder
- ½ teaspoon garlic powder

Directions:

- Heat the oven to 325°F.
- Put the rice cakes and crackers in a large bowl.
- In a small bowl, stir together the margarine, chili powder, and garlic powder. Pour over the rice-cake mixture, stirring to coat. Spread in a single layer on a baking sheet.
- Bake for 25 minutes, stirring and turning over once or twice. Serve or let cool completely and store at room temperature in an airtight container for up to two weeks

2.10 Sugar-and-Spice Snack Mix

Servings: 14 persons

Preparation time: 5 minutes

Cooking time: 25 minutes

Nutritional information: (Per Serving): Calories 121, Total Fat 1.5 g, Carbohydrates 25 g, Protein 2 g

Ingredients:

- 3 cups of lightly sweet, toasted oat cereal
- 3 cups of miniature no-salt pretzels
- 2 tablespoons of a light tub of margarine
- 1 tablespoon of firmly packed light brown sugar
- ½ teaspoon of ground cinnamon
- 1 cup mixed dried fruit bits

Directions:

- Heat the oven to 325°F.
- Put the cereal and pretzels in a large bowl.
- In a small bowl, stir together the margarine, brown sugar, and cinnamon. Pour over the cereal mixture, stirring to coat. Spread in a single layer on a large baking sheet.
- Bake for 25 minutes, stirring and turning over once or twice.
- Spread the mix on paper towels to cool for about 10 minutes. Transfer to an airtight container. Stir in the dried fruit. Serve or store at room temperature for up to two weeks

2.11 Homemade Corn Tortilla Chips

Servings: 8 persons

Preparation time: 5 minutes

Cooking time: 8 to 10 minutes

Nutritional information: (Per Serving): Calories 39, Total Fat 0.5 g, Carbohydrates 8 g, Protein 1 g

Ingredients:

- 10 6-inch corn tortillas
- Cooking spray
- ¼ teaspoon salt

Directions:

- Heat the oven to 450°F.
- Place 3 or 4 tortillas in a stack. Cut the stack into 4 wedges. Repeat with the remaining tortillas, making a total of 40 wedges. Arrange in a single layer on 2 baking sheets. Lightly spray with cooking oil spray. Sprinkle with salt.
- Bake for 8 to 10 minutes, or until crisp. Serve, or if storing, transfer to cooling racks and let cool for 5 to 10 minutes. Store at room temperature in an airtight container for up to two weeks

2.12 Banana-Kiwi Smoothies

Servings: 2 persons

Preparation time: 5 minutes

Cooking Time: 0 minutes

Nutritional information: (Per Serving): Calories 209, Total Fat 0.0 g, Carbohydrates 44 g, Protein 10 g

Ingredients:

- 1 medium banana, quartered
- 1 medium kiwifruit, peeled and quartered
- 1 cup fat-free milk
- 6 ounces fat-free fruit-flavored yogurt
- 2 teaspoons sugar

Directions:

- In a food processor or blender, process all the ingredients until smooth

2.13 Purple Slurp

Servings: 4 persons

Preparation time: 5 minutes

Cooking Time: 0 minutes

Nutritional information: (Per Serving): Calories 58, Total Fat 0.0 g, Carbohydrates 15 g, Protein 1 g

Ingredients:

- 1½ cups fresh or frozen unsweetened mixed berries or whole hulled strawberries
- 1 cup pomegranate juice (blueberry-pomegranate preferred)
- 1 cup ice cubes
- 1½ cups diet ginger ale

Directions:

- In a blender, process the berries, juice, and ice cubes until smooth. Stir in the ginger ale. Serve immediately.

2.14 Creamy Slurp

Servings: 4 persons

Preparation time: 5 minutes

Cooking Time: 0 minutes

Nutritional information: (Per Serving): Calories 93, Total Fat 0.0 g, Carbohydrates 22 g, Protein 2g

Ingredients:

- 1½ cups fresh or frozen unsweetened mixed berries or whole hulled strawberries
- 1 cup pomegranate juice (blueberry-pomegranate preferred)
- 1 cup ice cubes
- 1½ cups diet ginger ale

Directions:

- In a blender, process the berries, juice, and ice cubes until smooth. Stir in the ginger ale. Serve immediately.

Chapter 3 Soups

While certain soups may destroy a diet (cream-based types are especially heavy in fat and calories), the majority can help you achieve your daily vegetable intake. Consider soups a chance to capitalizeon nature's abundance (winter vegetables such as pumpkin, butternut squash, carrots, and parsnips will not wilt or go limp when cooked). If you have vegetables thatareready to go bad, putting theminto a soup dish might give them new life. You may even add frozen veggies to theboiling soup without sacrificing flavoror texture. Soups and stews don't need a lot of hands-on time. In reality, withthe Instant Pot, you can make a flavorful soup in five minutes and leave the rest inthe cooker. If you increase the quantity of liquid and veggies, you may use less costly items like chicken, fish, and meat. Make it a meal by serving it with whole-grain bread and a small salad, if desired. It›s fairly unusual to drink less than you need during the winter weather. However, even if you are not hot and sweaty, you still lose fluid from regular activity. Soups are an excellent method to remain hydrated and full since they are primarily liquid. Soups may help you avoid colds and flu, and they›re also a terrific remedy when you›re ill! Most soups are high in anti-inflammatory ingredients. Studies suggest that chicken soup, particularly when loaded with fresh garlic, onions, celery, and carrots, may help avoid the common cold. (They are all high in immune-boosting compounds.) An added benefit is that the heated drink soothes a sore throat.

3.1 Skillet-Roasted Bell Pepper, Zucchini, and Vermicelli Soup

Servings: 4 persons

Preparation time: 8 to 10 minutes

Cooking Time: 13 to 15 minutes

Nutritional information: (Per Serving): Calories 136, Total Fat 7.5 g, Carbohydrates 14 g, Protein 4 g

Ingredients:

- 3 cups fat-free, low-sodium chicken broth
- 1/8 teaspoon crushed red pepper flakes
- 2 ounces uncooked whole-grain vermicelli or whole-grain thin spaghetti, broken into 2-inch pieces
- 1 teaspoon olive oil and 1 tablespoon plus 2 teaspoons olive oil (extra-virgin preferred), divided use
- 1 medium red bell pepper, chopped
- 1 medium zucchini, chopped
- ½ cup water
- 2 tablespoons chopped fresh basil or 2 teaspoons dried, crumbled
- 1/8 teaspoon salt

Directions:

- Bring the broth and red pepper flakes to a boil in a large pot over high heat.
- Remove from heat. Add the spaghetti and toss well to combine everything. Return to the boil. Simmer for 10 minutes, covered, or till the pasta is al dente.
- Pour 1 teaspoon of oil into a nonstick pan over medium-high heat and swirl it around

to coat the bottom. 6 minutes of cooking time for the bell pepper and zucchini should be enough, with frequent stirring. Do not continue to cook.

- Scrape the bottom and side of the pan with a spatula as you add the water, being sure to remove any burnt parts. The leftover liquid should be protected from evaporation by covering the area. Set away for later.
- Add the bell pepper combination, basil, salt, and the remaining 1 tablespoon + 2 tablespoons of oil to the pasta when it is done.

3.2 Puréed Broccoli Soup with Lemon-Infused Oil

Servings: 4 persons

Preparation time: 8 minutes

Cooking Time: 7 minutes

Nutritional information: (Per Serving): Calories 83, Total Fat 5.0 g, Carbohydrates 7 g, Protein 4 g

Ingredients:

- 1 tablespoon plus 1 teaspoon olive oil (extra-virgin preferred)
- 2 teaspoons grated lemon zest
- 1 tablespoon fresh lemon juice
- 1/8 teaspoon salt
- Cooking spray
- ¼ cup plus 2 tablespoons very finely chopped green onions and 2 tablespoons chopped green onions, divided use
- 3 cups fat-free, low-sodium chicken broth
- 12 ounces fresh or frozen broccoli florets, thawed
- 1/8 teaspoon cayenne

Directions:

- In a small bowl, stir together the topping ingredients. Put aside.
- Lightly spray a large saucepan with cooking oil spray. Cook ¼ cup plus 2 tablespoons green onions over high heat for 1 minute, stirring once or twice.
- Pour the broth into the pan. Increase the heat to high and bring the mixture to a boil. Stir in the broccoli and cayenne. Return to a boil. Reduce the heat and simmer, covered, for 2 to 3 minutes, or till the broccoli is just tender.
- In a food processor or blender, process the soup in batches until smooth. Transfer to bowls.
- Stir the topping mixture. Drizzle over each serving, but don't stir it into the soup. Sprinkle with the remaining 2 tablespoons green onions

3.3 Double-Tomato Soup

Servings: 6 persons

Preparation time: 10 minutes

Cooking Time: 22 minutes

Nutritional information: (Per Serving): Calories 71, Total Fat 2.0 g, Carbohydrates 10 g, Protein 2 g

Ingredients:

- 2 teaspoons olive oil
- 1 small carrot, chopped
- 1 small rib of celery, chopped
- ¼ cup chopped onion
- ½ teaspoon of bottled minced garlic
- 2 14.5-ounce cans of no-salt-added diced tomatoes, undrained
- 2 cups water
- 8 dry-packed sun-dried tomato halves, chopped
- 1/8 teaspoon dried oregano, crumbled
- 1/8 teaspoon dried basil, crumbled
- Pinch of pepper
- 2 tablespoons shredded or grated Parmesan cheese

Directions:

- In a large saucepan, heat the oil over medium-high heat, swirling to coat the bottom. Cook

the carrot, celery, onion, and garlic for 3 minutes, stirring frequently.
- Stir in the remaining ingredients except for the Parmesan. Increase the heat to high and bring it to a boil. Reduce the heat and simmer, covered, for 15 minutes, or till the vegetables are tender. Serve the soup sprinkled with Parmesan.

3.4 Spinach and Brown Rice Soup with Ginger

Servings: 6 persons

Preparation time: 13 minutes

Cooking Time: 4 minutes

Nutritional information: (Per Serving): Calories 59, Total Fat 1.0 g, Carbohydrates 7 g, Protein 6 g

Ingredients:

- cups fat-free, low-sodium chicken broth
- 5 ounces frozen cooked brown rice (about 1 cup)
- 2 teaspoons bottled minced garlic or 4 medium garlic cloves, minced
- ¼ teaspoon crushed red pepper flakes
- ¾ ounce spinach, coarsely chopped (about ¾ cup)
- ½ cup diced cooked chicken breast, cooked without salt
- ½ cup finely chopped yellow bell pepper
- 3 tablespoons chopped fresh basil (optional)
- 1 tablespoon minced peeled gingerroot
- 1 teaspoonsoy sauce (lowest sodium available)
- 1/8teaspoon salt
- ½ cup snipped fresh cilantro or finely chopped green onions (cilantro preferred

Directions:

- In a large saucepan, bring the broth, rice, garlic, and red pepper flakes to a boil over high heat. Remove from the heat.
- Stir in the remaining ingredients except for the cilantro. Sprinkle with the cilantro.

3.5 Mushroom-Asparagus Chowder

Servings: 6 persons

Preparation time: 7 minutes

Cooking Time: 15 minutes

Nutritional information: (Per Serving): Calories 98, Total Fat 0.5 g, Carbohydrates 16 g, Protein 9 g

Ingredients:

- cups fat-free, low-sodium chicken broth
- ¼ teaspoon salt
- ¼ teaspoon ground nutmeg
- 1/8teaspoon pepper
- 1 pound asparagus, trimmed and cut on the diagonal into 1-inch pieces
- 8 ounces pre-sliced button mushrooms (about 2½ cups)
- 12 ounces fat-free evaporated milk
- ¼ cup all-purpose flour

Directions:

- In a large saucepan, bring the broth, salt, nutmeg, and pepper to a boil over high heat.
- Stir in the asparagus and mushrooms. Return to a boil. Reduce the heat and simmer, covered, for 5 minutes, or till the asparagus is just tender.
- Meanwhile, in a small bowl, whisk the milk and flour. When the asparagus is ready, pour the milk mixture into the soup.
- Cook over medium heat for 6 minutes, or until thickened and bubbly, stirring frequently.

3.6 Peppery Pumpkin Soup

Servings: 6 persons

Preparation time: x5 minutes

Cooking Time: 15 minutes

Nutritional information: (Per Serving): Calories 87, Total Fat 0.5 g, Carbohydrates 15 g, Protein 7 g

Ingredients:

- 1 15-ounce can solid-pack pumpkin (not pie filling)
- 1¼ cups fat-free, low-sodium chicken broth
- ¼ teaspoon onion powder
- 1/8 to ¼ teaspoon pepper
- 1/8 teaspoon salt
- 1/8 teaspoon ground nutmeg
- 1 12-ounce can fat-free evaporated milk
- ¼ cup fat-free sour cream
- 1 tablespoon unsalted shelled pumpkin seeds (optional)

Directions:

- In a saucepan, stir together the pumpkin, broth, onion powder, pepper, salt, and nutmeg. Cook over high heat for 10 minutes, or until bubbly, stirring occasionally.
- Stir in the milk. Cook for 5 minutes, or until heated through; don't let the soup come to a boil. Serve with dollops of sour cream and a sprinkling of pumpkin seeds.

3.7 Chilled Strawberry-Cantaloupe Soup

Servings: 4 persons

Preparation time: 10 minutes

Cooking Time: 0 minutes

Nutritional information: (Per Serving): Calories 102, Total Fat 0.5 g, Carbohydrates 23 g, Protein 3 g

Ingredients:

- ½ medium cantaloupe, cut into chunks (about 2 cups), chilled
- 1 cup hulled strawberries or raspberries, chilled
- 1 small banana, cut into chunks
- ½ cup unsweetened pineapple juice, chilled
- ½ cup fat-free vanilla yogurt, chilled

Directions:

- In a food processor or blender, process all the ingredients except the yogurt until smooth.
- Add the yogurt. Process until combined. Serve or refrigerate in an airtight container for up to 24 hours.

3.8 Curried Shrimp Bisque

Servings: 6 persons

Preparation time: 15 to 20 minutes

Cooking Time: 23 to 28 minutes

Nutritional information: (Per Serving): Calories 196, Total Fat 1.0 g, Carbohydrates 31 g, Protein 18 g

Ingredients:

- Cooking spray
- 2 medium apples, peeled and chopped
- 1 cup chopped onion
- ½ cup pre-shredded carrot
- 1 medium rib of celery, sliced
- 2 cups fat-free, low-sodium chicken broth
- 2 medium baking potatoes, peeled and diced
- 2 tablespoons curry powder
- ¼ teaspoon ground cardamom
- ¼ teaspoon ground allspice
- ¼ teaspoon salt
- 1 cup fat-free half-and-half
- ¼ cup no-salt-added tomato sauce
- 1 pound frozen peeled raw medium shrimp, rinsed
- Snipped fresh cilantro (optional)

Directions:

- Lightly spray a large saucepan with cooking oil spray. Cook the apples, onion, carrot, and

celery over high heat for 5 minutes, or till the apples are tender, stirring frequently.
- Stir in the broth, potatoes, curry powder, cardamom, allspice, and salt. Bring to a boil. Reduce the heat and simmer, covered, for 10 minutes, or till the potatoes are tender.
- In a food processor or blender, process the soup plus the half-and-half and tomato sauce in batches until smooth. Return the soup to the pan.
- Bring the soup to a boil over high heat. Stir in the shrimp. Reduce the heat and simmer for 3 to 5 minutes, or till the shrimp are pink. Serve garnished with cilantro.

3.9 Thirty-Minute Minestrone

Servings: 8 persons

Preparation time: 15 minutes

Cooking Time: 15 minutes

Nutritional information: (Per Serving): Calories 128, Total Fat 1.0 g, Carbohydrates 23 g, Protein 6 g

Ingredients:
- 4 cups water
- 2 cups baby carrots
- 1 15.5-ounce can reduced-sodium Great Northern beans, rinsed and drained
- 1 14.5-ounce can of unsalted diced tomatoes, undrained
- 1 cup chopped onion
- 1 tablespoon plus 1 teaspoon very low sodium beef bouillon granules
- 1 teaspoon of bottled minced garlic or 2 garlic cloves
- ½ teaspoon dried basil, crumbled
- ½ teaspoon of dried oregano, crushed
- ½ teaspoon pepper
- 9 or 10 ounces frozen Italian green beans
- 1 small zucchini, halved lengthwise and sliced crosswise
- ½ cup dried whole-grain elbow macaroni or broken dried whole-grain spaghetti
- ¼ cup shredded or grated Parmesan cheese

Directions:
- Cook the carrots and Great Northern beans in a large shallow pan with the bouillon granules, onion, garlic, basil, oregano and pepper. Over high heat, bring to a rolling boil.
- Mix in the spaghetti, green beans, and zucchini. Return to the boil. Simmer the pasta for 10 minutes with the lid on, or until al dente. To serve, top with Parmesan cheese.

3.10 Rosemary-Lemon Vegetable Soup

Servings: 4 persons

Preparation time: 12 minutes

Cooking Time: 24 minutes

Nutritional information: (Per Serving): Calories 266, Total Fat 3.5 g, Carbohydrates 48 g, Protein 11 g

Ingredients:
- 1 teaspoon olive oil
- 1 medium onion, chopped
- 1 teaspoon bottled minced garlic or 2 medium garlic cloves, minced
- 2 14.5-ounce cans of no-salt-added diced tomatoes, undrained
- 1 15.5-ounce can no-salt-add small red beans, rinsed and drained
- 2 cups low-sodium vegetable broth
- 1 large carrot, chopped
- 1 medium rib of celery, chopped
- ½ cup uncooked amaranth
- 2 tablespoons no-salt-added tomato paste
- 2 teaspoons finely snipped fresh rosemary
- 1 teaspoon grated lemon zest
- 2 teaspoons fresh lemon juice
- ¼ teaspoon pepper
- ¼ teaspoon salt

Directions:

- In a large saucepan, heat the oil over medium-high heat, swirling to coat the bottom. Brown the onions for 2 minutes, or until almost soft, stirring frequently.
- Stir in the garlic. Cook for 1 minute, stirring frequently.
- Stir in the tomatoes with liquid, beans, broth, carrot, celery, amaranth, and tomato paste. Bring to a boil, still over medium-high heat. Reduce the heat and simmer, covered, for 15 minutes, or till the amaranth is tender. Remove from the heat.
- Stir in the remaining ingredients. Serve immediately, so theamaranth doesn't continue to absorb liquid and make the soup too thick.

Directions:

- In a large saucepan, cook the beef, carrot, onion, cumin, oregano, garlic, and cayenne over high heat for 8 minutes, or till the beef is browned on the outside and no longer pink in the center, occasionally stirring to turn and break up the beef.
- Stir in the broth, tomatoes with liquid, and rice. Increase the heat to high and bring it to a boil. Reduce the heat and simmer, covered, for 5 minutes.
- Stir in the squash and simmer, covered, for 5 minutes, or till the squash is tender-crisp. Stir in the cilantro and lime juice.

3.11 Beef and Vegetable Soup with Cilantro and Lime

Servings: 4 persons

Preparation time: 10 to 12 minutes

Cooking Time: 21 minutes

Nutritional information: (Per Serving): Calories 178, Total Fat 3.5 g, Carbohydrates 20 g, Protein 17

Ingredients:

- 8 ounces extra-lean ground beef
- 1 small carrot, chopped
- 1 small onion, chopped
- 2 teaspoons of ground cumin
- ½ teaspoon of dried oregano, crumbled
- ½ teaspoon of bottled minced garlic
- 1/8 teaspoon of cayenne
- 3½ cups fat-free, no-salt-added beef broth
- 1 14.5-ounce can no-salt-add diced tomatoes, undrained
- ½ cup of uncooked instant brown rice
- 1 small yellow summer squash, chopped
- ¼ cup of snipped fresh cilantro
- 2 tablespoons of fresh lime juice

Chapter 4 Salads

Eating a salad every day is associated with better nutritional levels. The addition of vinaigrette to a salad helps to boost the uptake of certain nutrients that are absorbed by the body. Salad dressing contains fat, which aids in the absorption of important nutrients such as carotenoid and alpha- and beta-carotene. People who consume salads, salad dressings, and fresh veggies are more likely to reach the required daily intakes of vitamins C, E, and folic acid, according to the American Dietetic Association. Pre-menopausal weight loss in women has also been shown to be reduced in women who consume a lot of fruits and vegetables. Having one dish of salad or fresh veggies per day increases the chance of attaining the required nutritional intakes for nutrients A, E, Vitamin b, and folic by a large margin.

4.1 Strawberry-Spinach Salad with Champagne Dressing

Servings: 4 persons

Preparation time: 15 minutes

Cooking Time: 4 minutes

Nutritional information: (Per Serving): Calories 94, Total Fat 4.5 g, Carbohydrates 11 g, Protein 3 g

Ingredients:

For Dressing

- 3 tablespoons of brut champagne or white wine vinegar
- 1 tablespoon all-fruit strawberry spread
- 1 teaspoon of canola

For Salad

- 5 ounces spinach, torn into bite-size pieces (about 5 cups)
- 2 cups of halved hulled strawberries
- ¼ cup sliced almonds, dry-roasted

Directions:

In a small bowl, whisk the dressing ingredients.

In a large bowl, gently toss together the spinach and strawberries. Pour the dressing over the salad, gently tossing to coat. Sprinkle with the almonds.

4.2 Mustard-Marinated Vegetable Salad

Servings: 6 persons

Preparation time: 12 minutes

Cooking Time: 30 minutes

Nutritional information: (Per Serving): Calories 67, Total Fat 3.5 g, Carbohydrates 6 g, Protein 1 g

Ingredients:

For Salad

- 14 to 16 ounces frozen mixed vegetables, such as cauliflower florets, baby brussels sprouts, broccoli florets, and carrots
- 1 small yellow summer squash, sliced (optional)

For Dressing

- 3 tablespoons fresh orange juice
- 2 tablespoons of cider vinegar
- 2 tablespoons of olive oil (extra-virgin preferred)
- 1 tablespoon Dijon mustard (lowest sodium available)
- ½ teaspoon bottled minced garlic or 1 medium garlic clove, minced
- ¼ teaspoon of dried tarragon, crumbled
- ¼ teaspoon of dried marjoram, crumbled
- 1/2 teaspoon salt
- 1/8 teaspoon pepper

Directions:

- In a glass dish, such as an 8-inch square, stir together the salad ingredients, breaking them apart if necessary.
- In a small bowl, whisk the dressing ingredients. Pour over the vegetables, tossing to coat. Let stand, covered, at room temperature for 3 hours to 3 hours 30 minutes, or till the frozen vegetables are thawed, stirring occasionally. If you prefer to serve the salad chilled, refrigerate for about 30 minutes, continuing to stir occasionally.

4.3 No-Chop Cajun Coleslaw

Servings: 6 persons

Preparation time: 5 minutes

Cooking Time: 0 minutes

Nutritional information: (Per Serving): Calories 63, Total Fat 4.5 g, Carbohydrates 5 g, Protein 1 g

Ingredients:

- cups packaged shredded cabbage and carrot slaw
- ½ cup light mayonnaise
- 1 teaspoon of white wine vinegar or cider vinegar
- 2 teaspoons bottled white horseradish, drained
- ¼ teaspoon onion powder
- 1/8 teaspoon cayenne

Directions:

- Put the slaw in a large bowl.
- In a small bowl, whisk the remaining ingredients. Pour over the slaw, tossing to coat. Cover and refrigerate for 2 to 24 hours. Stir just before serving.

4.4 Grilled Pineapple with Zesty Blueberry Topping

Servings: 4 persons

Preparation time: 8 minutes

Cooking Time: 16 minutes

Nutritional information: (Per Serving): Calories 62, Total Fat 0.0 g, Carbohydrates 16 g, Protein 1 g

Ingredients:

- Cooking spray
- 4 ½-inch-thick slices of fresh pineapple
- 2 tablespoons raspberry vinegar
- 2 teaspoons sugar
- 1 teaspoon grated orange zest
- 1 cup fresh or frozen blueberries, thawed and patted dry if frozen
- 2 tablespoons finely chopped red onion

Directions:

- Lightly spray the grill rack with cooking oil spray. Preheat the grill to medium-high.
- Lightly spray both sides of the pineapple with cooking oil spray.
- Grill the pineapple for 3 minutes on each side, or until tender and begins to get richly brown. Transfer to a large plate. Refrigerate for 8 to 10 minutes to cool quickly, turning once halfway through.
- Meanwhile, in a small bowl, stir together the vinegar, sugar, and orange zest until the sugar is dissolved. Gently stir in the blueberries and onion. Spoon over the chilled pineapple.

4.5 Pasta and Sugar Snap Pea Salad

Servings: 4 persons

Preparation time: 10 to 12 minutes

Cooking Time: 20 minutes

Nutritional Information: (Per Serving): Calories 77, Total Fat 1.5 g, Carbohydrates 13 g, Protein 3 g

Ingredients:

- 2 ounces dried whole-grain penne (scant ¾ cup)
- 3 ounces sugar snap peas, trimmed (about 1 cup)

- 2 teaspoons soy sauce (lowest sodium available)
- 2 teaspoons plain rice vinegar
- 1 teaspoon of canola
- ¼ teaspoon grated peeled gingerroot
- ¼ medium red bell pepper, cut into short, thin strips
- ¼ small red onion, thinly sliced
- 1 tablespoon snipped fresh cilantro

Directions:

- Prepare the pasta using the package directions, omitting the salt and adding the peas during the last 2 minutes of cooking time.
- Transfer to a colander. Run under cold water for 1 to 2 minutes, or until cool. Drain well. Put aside.
- Meanwhile, in a small bowl, whisk the soy sauce, vinegar, oil, and ginger root. Put aside.
- In a large bowl, stir together the bell pepper, onion, and cilantro. Put aside.
- When the pasta mixture is cool, stir in the bell pepper mixture. Pour in the dressing, tossing to coat. Serve at room temperature for the best flavor.

4.6 Fresh Herb Potato Salad

Servings: 6 persons

Preparation time: 15 minutes

Cooking Time: 0 minutes

Nutritional information: (Per Serving): Calories 84, Total Fat 2.5 g, Carbohydrates 14 g, Protein 2 g

Ingredients:

- 1 15-ounce can unsalted whole potatoes, rinsed, drained, patted dry, and cut into bite-size pieces
- 1 medium carrot, sliced
- 1 medium rib of celery, sliced
- ½ cup frozen green peas (tiny preferred)
- ½ tablespoon of chopped shallot or green onion
- ¼ cup light mayonnaise
- 1½ teaspoons snipped fresh dillweed or ¼ teaspoon of dried, crumbled
- 1½ teaspoons snipped fresh basil or ¼ teaspoon of dried, crumbled
- 1 teaspoon Dijon mustard (lowest sodium available)
- 1 teaspoon white wine vinegar
- Pinch of pepper

Directions:

- In a large bowl, stir together the potatoes, carrots, celery, peas, and shallot.
- In a small bowl, whisk the remaining ingredients. Pour over the potato mixture, stirring to coat. Cover and refrigerate for 2 to 24 hours. Stir just before serving

4.7 Mediterranean Black Bean Salad

Servings: 4 persons

Preparation time: 10 to 12 minutes

Cooking Time: 21 minutes

Nutritional information: (Per Serving): Calories 84, Total Fat 1.0 g, Carbohydrates 15 g., Protein 5 g

Ingredients:

- 1 15.5-ounce can unsalted black beans, rinsed and drained
- 1 medium red, yellow, or orange bell pepper, chopped

- 1 medium green bell pepper, chopped
- 2 tablespoons chopped onion
- 2 tablespoons fat-free, low-sodium chicken broth
- 1/2 tablespoon of balsamic vinegar or red wine vinegar
- 1 teaspoon olive oil (extra-virgin preferred)
- ½ teaspoon bottled minced garlic or 1 medium garlic clove, minced
- ¼ teaspoon of dried thyme, crumbled
- ¼ teaspoon of dried rosemary, crushed
- 1/8 teaspoon pepper
- ¼ cup snipped fresh parsley

Directions:

- In a bowl, stir together the beans, bell peppers, and onion.
- In a small bowl, whisk the remaining ingredients except for the parsley. Pour over the bean mixture, tossing to coat. Stir in the parsley. Cover and refrigerate for 2 to 24 hours. Stir just before serving

4.8 Tabbouleh

Servings: 8 persons

Preparation time: 18 to 20 minutes

Cooking Time: 0 minutes

Nutritional information: (Per Serving): Calories 84, Total Fat 1.0 g, Carbohydrates 15 g, Protein 5 g

Ingredients:

Salad

- ¾ cup uncooked finebulgur
- ¾ cup boiling water
- 1 14.5-ounce can no-salt-add diced stewed tomatoes, undrained
- 1 cup snipped fresh parsley
- ½ cup snipped fresh mint
- ½ cup dried currants or raisins

Dressing

- ¼ cup fat-free, low-sodium chicken broth
- ¼ cup fresh lemon juice
- 2 tablespoons olive oil (extra-virgin preferred)
- ½ teaspoon curry powder
- ½ teaspoon ground cumin
- ½ teaspoon ground cinnamon
- ½ teaspoon bottled minced garlic or 1 medium garlic clove, minced

Directions:

- In a small bowl, stir together the bulgur and water. Put aside.
- In a large bowl, stir together the tomatoes with liquid, parsley, mint, and currants. Put aside.
- In a separate small bowl, whisk the dressing ingredients.
- Stir the bulgur mixture into the tomato mixture. Pour the dressing overall, tossing to coat. Cover and refrigerate for 2 to 24 hours (the bulgur will absorb the liquid during refrigeration). Stir just before serving.

4.9 Tuna Salad Bundles with Lemon and Dill

Servings: 4 persons

Preparation time: 10 to 15 minutes

Cooking Time: 0 minutes

Nutritional information: (Per Serving): Calories 131, Total Fat 1.5 g, Carbohydrates 7 g, Protein 26 g

Ingredients:

- 2 5-ounce cans of very low sodium white albacore tuna, packed in water, well-drained, and flaked
- 1 cup fat-free cottage cheese
- 2 to 3 medium green onions, sliced (about ¼ cup)
- 2 tablespoons snipped fresh dillweed or ¾ teaspoon dried, crumbled
- 1 teaspoon grated lemon zest
- ½ tablespoon of fresh lemon juice
- ¼ teaspoon of salt-free lemon pepper

- 1/8 teaspoon pepper
- 8 large romaine leaves

Directions:

- In a bowl, stir together all the ingredients except the romaine. Cover and refrigerate until serving time or proceed as directed.
- Spoon a generous 1/3 cup salad down the center of a romaine leaf, leaving about a half-inch uncovered at each end. Fold the sides of the leaf to the center and secure it with a wooden toothpick if desired. Repeat with the remaining salad and romaine

4.10 Warm Chicken and Papaya Salad

Servings: 4 persons

Preparation time: 10 to 12 minutes

Cooking Time: 21 minutes

Nutritional information: (Per Serving): Calories 201, Total Fat 9.0 g, Carbohydrates 11 g, Protein 19 g

Ingredients:

- 12 ounces boneless, skinless chicken tenders, all visible fat discarded
- 2 tablespoons fresh lime juice and 2 tablespoons fresh lime juice, divided use
- 4 ounces lettuce, such as romaine or mixed salad greens, torn into bite-size pieces (about 4 cups)
- 1-ounce radicchio or red leaf lettuce, torn into bite-size pieces (about 1 cup)
- 1 medium papaya, peeled, seeded, and cubed (about 1½ cups)
- 2 to 3 medium green onions, sliced (about ¼ cup)
- 2 tablespoons olive oil (extra-virgin preferred)
- 2 tablespoons fat-free, low-sodium chicken broth
- ½ teaspoon Dijon mustard (lowest sodium available)
- ½ teaspoon bottled minced garlic or 1 medium garlic clove, minced
- 1/8 teaspoon pepper

Directions:

- Put the chicken In a glass dish. Pour 2 tablespoons lime juice over the chicken, turning to coat. Put aside.
- In a large bowl, toss together the lettuce, radicchio, papaya, and green onions. Put aside.
- In a small bowl, whisk the oil, broth, mustard, garlic, pepper, and remaining 2 tablespoons lime juice. Put aside.
- Drain the chicken, discarding the marinade.
- Lightly spray a large pan with cooking oil spray. Heat over high heat. Cook the chicken for 3 to 5 minutes, or until no longer pink in the center, turning once halfway through. Transfer to a cutting board. Cut into bite-size pieces.
- Whisk the dressing and pour over the lettuce mixture, tossing to coat. Top with the chicken. Serve immediately for the best texture.

4.11 Melon-Chicken Salad

Servings: 4 persons

Preparation time: 15 to 20 minutes

Cooking Time: 7 minutes

Nutritional information: (Per Serving): Calories 219, Total Fat 6.0 g, Carbohydrates 21 g, Protein 21 g

Ingredients:

- 12 ounces boneless, skinless chicken breast tenders, all visible fat discarded
- 1 large or 2 small cantaloupes, cut into bite-size pieces
- 2 medium ribs of celery, sliced (about 1 cup)
- 2 tablespoons sliced green onions
- ¼ cup fat-free peach or vanilla yogurt
- ¼ cup light mayonnaise
- 4 large lettuce leaves, such as romaine or red lea

Directions:

- Pour water to a depth of 1 inch in a large skillet. Bring to a boil over high heat. Carefully add the chicken. Reduce the heat and simmer, covered, for 5 minutes, or till the chicken is no longer pink in the center. Drain well. Transfer to a cutting board. Put aside to cool slightly.
- Meanwhile, toss together the cantaloupe, celery, and green onions in a large bowl.
- When the chicken is cool enough to handle, cut it into bite-size pieces. Add to the cantaloupe mixture, tossing to combine.
- In a small bowl, whisk the yogurt and mayonnaise. Pour over the salad, tossing to coat. Serve immediately or cover and refrigerate until serving time. Just before serving, spoon the salad onto the lettuce leaves.

4.12 Speedy Taco Salad

Servings: 4 persons

Preparation time: 10 minutes

Cooking Time: 8 minutes

Nutritional information: (Per Serving): Calories 270, Total Fat 4.0 g, Carbohydrates 26 g, Protein 33 g

Ingredients:

- 12 ounces ground skinless turkey breast or chicken breast
- 1 15.5-ounce can no-salt-add red kidney beans, rinsed and drained
- 1 14.5-ounce can no-salt-add diced tomatoes, drained
- 1 4-ounce can chop green chiles, drained
- ½ tablespoon of chili powder
- 1 teaspoon ground cumin
- 5 ounces lettuce, such as romaine or red leaf, torn into bite-size pieces (about 5 cups)
- ½ cup shredded low-fat Mexican blend cheese

Directions:

- In a large skillet, cook the turkey over high heat for 5 minutes, or until browned on the outside and no longer pink in the center, occasionally stirring to turn and break up the turkey. Drain if needed.
- Stir in the beans, tomatoes, chiles, chili powder, and cumin. Reduce the heat to medium and cook for 2 minutes, stirring frequently.
- Put the lettuce on plates. Spoon the turkey mixture onto the lettuce. Sprinkle with the Mexican blend cheese. Serve immediately for the best texture

4.13 Pork and Water Chestnut Salad with Curry Dressing

Servings: 4 persons

Preparation time: 10 to 12 minutes

Cooking Time: 8-10 minutes

Nutritional information: (Per Serving): Calories 220, Total Fat 12.0 g, Carbohydrates 16 g, Protein 14 g

Ingredients:

- SALAD
- 1 teaspoon of canola or corn oil
- 8 ounces boneless center loin pork chops, all visible fat discarded, cut into ½-inch cubes
- 1 8-ounce can slice water chestnuts, drained and chopped
- 1/3 cup sweetened dried cranberries
- ¼ cup finely chopped red onion
- ¼ cup chopped pecans, dry-roasted

- DRESSING
- 2 tablespoons light mayonnaise
- 1 teaspoon curry powder
- ½ teaspoon ground cumin
- ¼ teaspoon of ground nutmeg
- ¼ teaspoon of salt
- 1/8 teaspoon crushed red pepper flakes (optional

Directions:

- In a nonstick pan, heat the oil over high heat, swirling to coat the bottom. Cook the pork for 5 minutes, or until slightly pink in the center and light golden brown on the edges, stirring occasionally. Spoon in a single layer onto a large plate. Refrigerate for 5 minutes to cool quickly.
- Meanwhile, In a bowl, stir together the remaining salad ingredients. Put aside.
- In a small bowl, whisk the dressing ingredients. Put aside.
- Stir the cooled pork and any accumulated juices into the salad mixture. Pour in the dressing, tossing to combine.

4.14 Layered Two-Bean Salad with Cheddar Cheese

Servings: 8 persons

Preparation time: 8 to 20 minutes

Cooking Time: 0 minutes

Nutritional information: (Per Serving); Calories 195, Total Fat 2.5 g, Carbohydrates 30 g, Protein 14 g

Ingredients:

- ounces lettuce, such as romaine or red leaf, torn into bite-size pieces (about 3 cups)
- 1 15.5-ounce can no-salt-added red kidney beans, rinsed and drained
- 1 15.5-ounce can no-salt-added black beans, rinsed and drained
- 8 ounces pre-sliced button mushrooms (about 2½ cups)
- 1 12-ounce can no-salt-added whole-kernel corn, drained
- ¼ cup chopped red onion
- 1 cup low-fat sour cream
- ¼ cup snipped fresh cilantro or parsley
- 2 tablespoons white wine vinegar
- ¼ teaspoon of salt
- 1/8 teaspoon pepper
- 1 cup shredded fat-free Cheddar cheese

Directions:

- Put the lettuce in a large shallow glass bowl or baking dish. In the order listed, make one layer each: kidney beans, black beans, mushrooms, corn, and onion.
- In a small bowl, whisk the remaining ingredients except for the Cheddar. Spread over the salad, all the way to the sides. Sprinkle with the Cheddar. Cover and refrigerate for 1 to 24 hours before serving

Chapter 5 Seafood

As a source of key nutrients such as omega-3 fats, A, and B vitamins, seafood is cholesterol-free-free, rich in protein, and low in fat overall. These nutrients are critical in the maintenance of your overall health, especially the health of your brain, eyes, and immune response. Because your system cannot create omega-3 fatty acids on its own, it is extremely vital to include seafood in your diet if you want to maintain your best health. Seafood may provide a much-needed boost to your brain's performance while also improving long-term brain health. In addition to lowering the chance of acquiring Alzheimer's disease, omega-3 fatty acids may help prevent theonset of dementia as you age. These nutrients also assist your body in maintaining optimal memory and mood regulation. Fish (particularly salmon) isvery abundant in omega-3 fatty acids, which are essential for heart health. It is recommended that you consume fish either once- or twice a week to boost your cardiovascular health and reducethe risk of heart attack and stroke. To ensure that you get all of the necessary nutrients for your health, eat a variety of fish every week.

In addition, if you often wake up with tight joints in the morning, you may want extra seafood in your diet. Seafood contains omega-3 fatty acids, which have anti-inflammatory properties that may be beneficial to persons who suffer from joint discomfort. It has been shown that eating seafood, particularly fatty fishmay help to lessen joint stiffness and the signs of arthritis.

5.1 Pasta-Crusted Fish with Marinara Sauce

Servings: 4 persons

Preparation time: 10 minutes

Cooking Time: 8 to 10 minutes

Nutritional information: (Per Serving): Calories 212, Total Fat 2.0 g, Carbohydrates 25 g, Protein 23 g

Ingredients:

- Cooking spray
- 1 cup finely chopped uncooked fresh angel hair pasta
- 4mild white fish fillets (about 4 ounces each), rinsed and patted dry
- ¼ teaspoon dried dillweed, crumbled
- Pepper to taste
- 1 cup marinara sauce (lowest sodium available

Directions:

- Cooking spray
- 1 cup finely chopped uncooked fresh angel hair pasta
- 4mild white fish fillets (about 4 ounces each), rinsed and patted dry
- ¼ teaspoon dried dillweed, crumbled
- Pepper to taste
- 1 cup marinara sauce (lowest sodium available

5.2 Pecan-Coated Fillets with Corn Relish

Servings: 4 persons

Preparation time: 10 minutes

Cooking Time: 10 to 15 minutes

Nutritional information: (Per Serving): Calories 215, Total Fat 9.5 g, Carbohydrates 14 g, Protein 20 g

Ingredients:

- Cooking spray

- 1 cup drained canned no-salt-added whole-kernel corn
- ½ medium green bell pepper, chopped
- ¼ cup chopped red onion
- 2 tablespoons snipped fresh cilantro or parsley
- 2 tablespoons fresh lime juice
- ½ teaspoon bottled minced garlic or 1 medium garlic clove, minced
- 1/8 teaspoon cayenne
- 1/8 teaspoon salt
- 4 mild white fish fillets (about 4 ounces each), rinsed and patted dry
- 2 tablespoons light mayonnaise
- Pepper to taste
- 1/3 cup chopped pecans, dry-roasted

Directions:

- Turn the oven on and set it to 450 degrees Fahrenheit. Lightly coat a deep glassware baking dish big enough to contain the fish in a single layer with cooking spray.
- In a mixing bowl, combine the corn, bell pepper, onion, cilantro, lime juice, garlic, cayenne pepper, and salt. Set aside for now.
- Arrange the fish in the baking dish, tucking the thin edges under to ensure uniform cooking. Brush the top of the fish lightly with the mayonnaise. Season with pepper and pecans.
- Bake for 10–15 minutes, or until the salmon flakes easily with a fork. Serve with pleasure.

5.3 Fish and Fettuccine

Servings: 4 persons

Preparation time: 10 minutes

Cooking Time: 35 to 40 minutes

Nutritional information: (Per Serving): Calories 318, Total Fat 3.5 g, Carbohydrates 41 g, Protein 29 g

Ingredients:

- 1 14.5-ounce can no-salt-add diced stewed tomatoes, undrained
- 4 mild white fish fillets (about 4 ounces each), rinsed and patted dry
- 1 9-ounce package uncooked fresh spinach fettuccine, coarsely chopped
- 2 small yellow summer squash, sliced
- 2 tablespoons chopped shallots
- 2 tablespoons snipped fresh basil or 1 teaspoon dried, crumbled
- 2 tablespoons snipped fresh oregano or 1 teaspoon dried, crumbled
- 1 teaspoon of salt
- 2 tablespoons shredded or grated Parmesan or Romano cheese

Directions:

- Heat the oven to 425°F.
- Pour the tomatoes with liquid into a 9-inch square glass baking dish. Make one layer each of the fish, pasta, summer squash, shallots, basil, and oregano. Sprinkle with salt.
- Bake, tightly covered, for 35 to 40 minutes, or till the fish flakes easily when tested with a fork. Remove from the oven. Sprinkle with the Parmesan. Let stand, covered, for 5 minutes before serving

5.4 Creole Catfish

Servings: 4 persons

Preparation time: 12 to 15 minutes

Cooking Time: 17 minutes

Nutritional information: (Per Serving): Calories 34, Total Fat 4.5 g, Carbohydrates 7 g, Protein 20 g

Ingredients:

- 2 teaspoons paprika
- ¼ teaspoon of salt
- ¼ teaspoon pepper
- Pinch of cayenne
- 1 teaspoon olive oil
- ½ medium rib of celery, diced
- ¼ medium red bell pepper, diced
- ¼ cup diced onion

- ½ teaspoon bottled minced garlic or 1 medium garlic clove, minced
- 1 14.5-ounce can no-salt-add diced tomatoes, undrained

Directions:

- Preheat the broiler. Line a baking sheet with aluminum foil. Lightly spray the foil with cooking oil spray. Put aside.
- In a small dish, stir together the paprika, salt, pepper, and cayenne. Put aside.
- In a skillet, heat the oil over medium-high heat, swirling to coat the bottom. Cook the celery, bell pepper, onion, and garlic for 3 minutes, stirring frequently.
- Stir in the tomatoes with liquid. Using a potato masher, mash the vegetables to make the sauce somewhat smoother.
- Stir in 1½ teaspoons of the paprika mixture, setting the remaining mixture aside. Bring the sauce to a boil. Reduce the heat and simmer for 10 minutes, or till the vegetables are tender and the sauce is thickened.
- Meanwhile, sprinkle the fish on both sides with the remaining 1 teaspoon paprika mixture. Using your fingertips, gently press the seasonings, so they adhere to the fish. Transfer to the baking sheet.
- Broil on one side about 4 inches from the heat for 8 minutes, or till the fish flakes easily when tested with a fork. Cut each fillet in half. Serve topped with the sauce.

5.5 Crunchy Fish Nuggets with Lemon Tartar Sauce

Servings: 4 persons

Preparation time: 15 minutes

Cooking Time: 5 minutes

Nutritional information: (Per Serving): Calories 245, Total Fat 11.0 g, Carbohydrates 7 g, Protein 28 g

Ingredients:

- 2 large egg whites
- 2 tablespoons fat-free milk
- ¼ cup whole-wheat panko (Japanese breadcrumbs)
- ¼ cup shredded or grated Parmesan cheese
- ½ teaspoon paprika
- 1 pound halibut steaks or fillets, rinsed and patted dry, cut into 24 bite-size pieces
- ½ cup light mayonnaise
- 2 tablespoons finely chopped dill pickle
- 1 teaspoon grated lemon zest
- 1 teaspoon fresh lemon juice

Directions:

- Heat the oven to 450°F. Lightly spray a large baking sheet with cooking oil spray. Put aside.
- In a shallow dish, whisk together the egg whites and milk.
- In a separate medium shallow dish, stir together the panko, Parmesan, and paprika.
- Put the dishes and baking sheet in a row, assembly-line fashion. Working in batches and using a slotted spoon, put the fish in the egg white mixture, turning to coat and letting any excess drip off. Transfer to the panko mixture, turning to coat well and gently shaking off any excess. Transfer to the baking sheet, arranging the fish in a single layer.
- Bake for 5 minutes until the fish flakes easily when tested with a fork.
- Meanwhile, in a small bowl, stir together the tartar sauce ingredients. Serve with the fish.

5.6 Broiled Halibut with Chunky Tomato-Cream Sauce

Servings: 4 persons

Preparation time: 8 minutes

Cooking Time: 10 to 12 minutes

Nutritional information: (Per Serving): Calories 181, Total Fat 3.5 g, Carbohydrates 9 g, Protein 26 g

Ingredients:

- 2 halibut steaks (about 8 ounces each), about 1 inch thick, rinsed and patted dry
- 1 teaspoon olive oil
- Pepper to taste
- 1 14.5-ounce can no-salt-added stewed tomatoes, chopped, undrained
- ½ teaspoon bottled minced garlic or 1 medium garlic clove, minced
- ¼ cup fat-free sour cream
- 1 tablespoon of all-purpose flour
- 1 teaspoon dried Italian seasoning, crumbled
- ¼ teaspoon of salt

Directions:

- Preheat the broiler. Lightly spray a broiler pan and rack with cooking oil spray.
- Put the fish on the rack. Lightly brush the top of the fish with the oil. Sprinkle with pepper.
- Broil about 4 inches from the heat for 5 minutes. Turnover. Broil for 3 to 7 minutes, or till the fish flakes easily when tested with a fork. Cut each fish steak in half.
- Meanwhile, In a saucepan, stir together the tomatoes with liquid and the garlic. Cook over high heat for 5 minutes or until bubbly.
- In a small bowl, whisk the sour cream, flour, Italian seasoning, and salt. Stir into the tomato mixture. Cook for 4 to 5 minutes, or until bubbly and thickened to the desired consistency, whisking constantly.
- Serve the fish with the seasoned side up. Spoon the sauce over the fish.

5.7 Halibut with Green Tea Glaze

Servings: 4 persons

Preparation time: 10 minutes

Cooking Time: 21 minutes

Nutritional information: (Per Serving): Calories 162, Total Fat 2.5 g, Carbohydrates 10 g, Protein 24 g

Ingredients:

- 1 cup unsweetened green tea
- 2 tablespoons honey
- 2 tablespoons fresh lime juice
- ¼ cup loosely packed fresh mint
- ¼ teaspoon crushed red pepper flakes
- 4 halibut fillets (about 4 ounces each), rinsed and patted dry
- 1 medium lime, cut into 4 wedges

Directions:

- Preheat the broiler.
- In a saucepan, stir together the tea, honey, and lime juice. Bring to a boil over high heat. Boil for 8 minutes, or till the mixture is syrupy and reduced to about ¼ cup. Remove from the heat.
- Stir in the mint and red pepper flakes. Let steep for 1 minute. Discard the mint.
- Place the fish on a rimmed baking sheet. Drizzle 1 tablespoon of the glaze over the top of the fish. Set the remaining glaze aside.
- Broil the fish 4 to 6 inches from the heat for 4 minutes. Turn over. Drizzle 1 tablespoon of the glaze over the fish. Set the remaining glaze

aside. Broil for 4 to 5 minutes, or till the fish flakes easily when tested with a fork.
- Transfer the fish to plates. Drizzle the remaining glaze over the fish. Serve with the lime wedges to squeeze over the fish.

5.8 Grilled Salmon with Mango-Lime Cream Sauce

Servings: 4 persons

Preparation time: 15-20 minutes

Cooking Time: 8 minutes

Nutritional information: (Per Serving): Calories 168, Total Fat 4.5, Carbohydrates 5 g, Protein 26 g

Ingredients:
- 1/8 teaspoon salt
- 1/8 teaspoon pepper (white preferred)
- 4 salmon fillets (about 4 ounces each), rinsed and patted dry
- 1/3 cup coarsely chopped bottled mangoes; 1 tablespoon juice reserved
- ¼ cup fat-free sour cream
- ½ teaspoon grated lime zest
- 1 teaspoon fresh lime juice

Directions:
- Lightly spray the grill rack with cooking oil spray. Preheat the grill to medium-high.
- Sprinkle the salt and pepper over one side of the salmon. Using your fingertips, gently press them so they adhere to the fish.
- Grill with the seasoned side down for 5 minutes. Turnover. Grill for 2 to 3 minutes or to the desired doneness.
- Meanwhile, in a small bowl, whisk together all the sauce ingredients. Serve at room temperature or cover and refrigerate until serving time. Spoon over the fish

5.9 Jerked Salmon with Raspberry-Mint Salsa

Servings: 4 persons

Preparation time: 15 minutes

Cooking Time: 8 minutes

Nutritional information: (Per Serving): Calories 181, Total Fat 4.5 g, Carbohydrates 9 g, Protein 25 g

Ingredients:
- 1 1/3 cups fresh or frozen unsweetened raspberries, thawed if frozen
- ¼ cup finely chopped red onion
- 2 tablespoons snipped fresh mint
- 1½ teaspoons sugar
- ½ teaspoon grated orange zest
- 2 tablespoons fresh orange juice
- 1 teaspoon salt-free jerk seasoning blend
- ½ teaspoon pepper (coarsely ground preferred)
- ½ teaspoon of salt
- 4 salmon fillets with skin (about 5 ounces each), rinsed and patted dry

Directions:
- Lightly spray the grill rack with cooking oil spray. Preheat the grill to medium.
- Meanwhile, in a small bowl, stir together the salsa ingredients. Put aside.
- In a separate small bowl, stir together the seasoning blend, pepper, and salt. Sprinkle over the top and sides of the fish. Using your fingertips, gently press the seasonings, so they adhere to the fish.
- Grill the fish with the skin side down for 5 minutes. Turn it over. Grill for 2 to 3 minutes, or until cooked to the desired doneness. Serve with salsa.

5.10 Spinach-Topped Salmon

Servings: 4 persons

Preparation time: 8 minutes

Cooking Time: 18 minutes

Nutritional information: (Per Serving): Calories 193, Total Fat 5.0 g, Carbohydrates 3 g, Protein 28 g

Ingredients:

- 1½ cups water
- ½ cup dry white wine (regular or nonalcoholic) or water
- 2 medium green onions, sliced
- 1 medium-dried bay leaf
- 4 salmon fillets (about 4 ounces each), rinsed and patted dry
- 5 ounces frozen chopped spinach
- 1/8 teaspoon ground nutmeg
- ¼ cup shredded low-fat mozzarella cheese
- Pepper to taste
- 1 medium lemon, thinly sliced (optional)

Directions:

- Preheat the broiler. Lightly spray the broiler pan and rack with cooking oil spray. Put aside.
- In a large skillet, bring the water, wine, green onions, and bay leaf just to a boil over high heat. Using a large spatula, carefully add each piece of fish. Return to a boil. Reduce the heat and simmer, covered, for 8 to 10 minutes, or till the fish is the desired doneness. Transfer the fish to the broiler rack. Discard the cooking liquid. Pat the fish dry with paper towels.
- Meanwhile, prepare the spinach using the package directions. Drain well, squeezing out the moisture. Stir in the nutmeg. Spread over the fish.
- Sprinkle the mozzarella and pepper over the spinach.
- Broil about 4 inches from the heat for 1 to 2 minutes, or till the mozzarella melts. Garnish the fish with lemon.

5.11 Salmon and Brown Rice Bake

Servings: 4 persons

Preparation time: 7 minutes

Cooking Time: 35 minutes

Nutritional information: (Per Serving): Calories 186, Total Fat 3.0 g, Carbohydrates 30 g, Protein 12 g

Ingredients:

- 10 ounces frozen whole-kernel corn
- ¾ cup uncooked instant brown rice
- 1 6-ounce vacuum-sealed pouch boneless, skinless pink salmon, flaked
- 2/3 cup water
- 2 tablespoons sliced green onions
- ½ teaspoon very low sodium chicken bouillon granules
- ¼ teaspoon dried dillweed, crumbled
- 1/8 teaspoon salt
- ¼ cup shredded low-fat Cheddar cheese

Directions:

- Heat the oven to 375°F.
- In a 1½-quart glass casserole dish, stir together all the ingredients except the Cheddar.
- Bake, covered, for 30 minutes, or till the rice is tender. Sprinkle with the Cheddar. Bake, uncovered, for 5 minutes, or till the Cheddar is melted.

5.12 Spicy Sole and Tomatoes

Servings: 4 persons

Preparation time: 8 minutes

Cooking Time: 10 to 12 minutes

Nutritional information: (Per Serving): Calories 136, Total Fat 1.5 g, Carbohydrates 7 g, Protein 22 g

Ingredients:

- ½ cup chopped onion
- ½ teaspoon bottled minced garlic or 1 medium garlic clove, minced
- 1 14.5-ounce can no-salt-add diced tomatoes, undrained
- 1 teaspoon capers, drained
- 4 peppercorns

- 4 to 6 dashes of red hot-pepper sauce, or to taste
- 4 sole or other mild white fish fillets (about 4 ounces each), rinsed and patted dry

Directions:

- Lightly spray a large pan with cooking oil spray. Brown the onion and garlic over high heat for 3 minutes, or till the onion is soft, stirring frequently.
- Stir in the remaining ingredients except for the fish. Bring to a boil.
- Place the fish in the tomato mixture. Return to a boil. Reduce the heat and simmer, covered, for 4 to 6 minutes, or till the fish flakes easily when tested with a fork. Discard the peppercorns before serving the fish.

5.13 Baked Tilapia with Pineapple Reduction

Servings: 4 persons

Preparation time: 8 minutes

Cooking Time: 8 minutes

Nutritional information: (Per Serving): Calories 183, Total Fat 5.5 g, Carbohydrates 9 g, Protein 23 g

Ingredients:

- 4 tilapia or other mild white fish fillets (about 4 ounces each), rinsed and patted dry
- 1 tablespoon canola or corn oil
- ¼ teaspoon pepper
- 1/8 teaspoon cayenne (optional)
- 2 tablespoons soy sauce (lowest sodium available)
- 1 tablespoon cider vinegar
- 2 teaspoons sugar
- 1½ teaspoons cornstarch
- ½ teaspoon curry powder
- 1/8 teaspoon crushed red pepper flakes (optional)
- ¾ cup pineapple juice

Directions:

- Heat the oven to 450°F. Line a baking sheet with aluminum foil. Lightly spray the foil with cooking oil spray.
- Place the fish on the baking sheet. Brush the top of the fish with the oil. Sprinkle the top with pepper and cayenne. Using your fingertips, gently press the seasonings, so they adhere to the fish.
- Bake for 8 minutes, or till the fish flakes easily when tested with a fork.
- Meanwhile, in a small bowl, whisk the sauce ingredients except for the pineapple juice until the corn-starch is dissolved. Put aside.
- In a large saucepan, bring the pineapple juice to a boil over high heat. Boil for 2 to 3 minutes, or until reduced to 1/3 cup. Whisk the soy sauce mixture into the pineapple juice. Reduce the heat to medium-high and cook for 1 minute, or till the mixture is slightly thickened, whisking frequently. Serve over the fish

5.14 Tex-Mex Tilapia Packets

Servings: 4 persons

Preparation time: 15 minutes

Cooking Time: 10 minutes

Nutritional information: (Per Serving): Calories 189, Total Fat 5.5 g, Carbohydrates 11 g, Protein 25 g

Ingredients:

- 1 medium lemon or lime, cut into 8 slices, and

- 1 medium lemon or lime, cut into 4 wedges, divided, use
- 4 tilapia or other mild white fish fillets (about 4 ounces each), rinsed and patted dry
- ¼ cup mild Picante sauce and ¼ cup mild Picante sauce (lowest sodium available), divided use
- 4 medium green onions, chopped
- 2 medium fresh jalapeños, seeds, and ribs discarded, finely chopped
- 1 tablespoon olive oil (extra-virgin preferred)
- ½ cup fat-free sour cream
- ¼ teaspoon pepper (coarsely ground preferred

Directions:

- Heat the oven to 425°F. Cut eight 12-inch square pieces of aluminum foil. Lightly spray one side of each with cooking oil spray.
- Place 2 lemon slices in the center of the sprayed side of four pieces of foil. Place the fish on the lemon slices. Top each serving with about 1 tablespoon Picante sauce. Sprinkle with green onions and jalapeños. Put one of the remaining pieces of foil with the sprayed side down over each serving. Fold the edges together several times to seal each packet securely, so the juices don't leak out. Transfer to a large baking sheet.
- Bake for 10 minutes. Using the tines of a fork, carefully open one of the packets away from you (to prevent steam burns). If the fish flakes easily when tested with the fork, it is done, and you can then carefully open the remaining packets. If the fish in the opened packet isn't cooked enough, reseal the packet and continue baking all the packets for about 2 minutes.
- Meanwhile, in a small bowl, stir together the oil and the remaining ¼ cup picante sauce. Spoon 1 tablespoon of the mixture over each serving. Top each with 2 tablespoons sour cream. Sprinkle with pepper. Serve the remaining lemon wedges to squeeze over the fish.

5.15 Broiled Tilapia with Black Bean Salsa

Servings: 4 persons

Preparation time: 10 minutes

Cooking Time: 10 minutes

Nutritional information: (Per Serving): Calories 226, Total Fat 2.0 g, Carbohydrates 22 g, Protein 29 g

Ingredients:

- 4 tilapia or other mild white fish fillets (about 4 ounces each), rinsed and patted dry
- 1 medium lime, halved crosswise, divided use
- 1 15.5-ounce can no-salt-add black beans, about 1 inch of liquid drained off
- 4 medium green onions, sliced
- 1 medium rib of celery, chopped
- 1 medium carrot, chopped
- 1 teaspoon ground cumin
- ½ teaspoon bottled minced garlic or 1 medium garlic clove, minced
- ¼ teaspoon minced fresh jalapeño, seeds and ribs discarded
- ¼ cup snipped fresh cilantro or parsley (optional)
- ¼ teaspoon salt

Directions:

- Preheat the broiler. Lightly spray a broiler pan and rack with cooking oil spray.
- Put the fish on the rack. Squeeze the juice from one lime half over the fish.
- Broil the fish about 4 inches from the heat for 4 minutes. Turn over. Squeeze the juice from the remaining lime half over the fish. Broil for 2 to 4 minutes, or till the fish flakes easily when tested with a fork.
- Meanwhile, in a saucepan, cook the beans and remaining liquid, green onions, celery, carrot, cumin, garlic, and jalapeño over medium-low

heat for 6 to 8 minutes, or till the fish is done, stirring occasionally. Stir in the cilantro and salt. Spoon over the fish.

5.16 Grilled Trout with Creamy Caper-Dill Sauce

Servings: 4 persons

Preparation time: 10 minutes

Cooking Time: 8 minutes

Nutritional information: (Per Serving): Calories 182, Total Fat 7.5 g, Carbohydrates 2 g, Protein 26 g

Ingredients:

- ½ cup fat-free Greek yogurt
- 2 tablespoons capers, drained and chopped
- 1½ teaspoons snipped fresh dillweed or ½ teaspoon dried, crumbled
- ½ teaspoon bottled minced garlic or 1 medium garlic clove, minced
- ¾ teaspoon snipped fresh oregano or ¼ teaspoon dried, crumbled
- 1/8 teaspoon salt
- 4 trout fillets (about 4 ounces each), rinsed and patted dry
- 1 tablespoon olive oil
- ½ teaspoon pepper (coarsely ground preferred)
- 1/8 teaspoon salt

Directions:

- Lightly spray the grill rack with cooking oil spray. Preheat the grill to medium.
- In a small bowl, whisk the sauce ingredients. Put aside.
- Brush both sides of the fish with the oil. Sprinkle with the pepper and remaining 1/8 teaspoon salt.
- Grill for 3 minutes. Carefully turn over. Grill for 3 to 5 minutes, or till the fish flakes easily when tested with a fork. Serve with the sauce.

5.17 Smoky Trout with Citrus Topping

Servings: 4 persons

Preparation time: 8 minutes

Cooking Time: 8 minutes

Nutritional information: (Per Serving): Calories 173, Total Fat 7.5 g, Carbohydrates 0 g, Protein 23 g

Ingredients:

- 1 teaspoon salt-free grilling seasoning blend
- ½ teaspoon smoked paprika
- ¼ teaspoon salt
- 4 trout fillets (about 4 ounces each), rinsed and patted dry
- 3 tablespoons light tub of any margarine
- 1½ teaspoons Louisiana hot sauce
- ½ teaspoon grated orange zest

Directions:

- Lightly spray the grill rack with cooking oil spray. Preheat the grill to medium.
- In a small bowl, stir together the seasoning blend, paprika, and salt.
- Lightly spray the fish on both sides with cooking oil spray. Sprinkle all over with the seasoning blend mixture. Using your fingertips, gently press the seasonings, so they adhere to the fish.
- Grill for 3 minutes. Carefully turn over. Grill for 3 to 5 minutes, or till the fish flakes easily when tested with a fork.
- Meanwhile, in a small microwaveable bowl, microwave the margarine on 100 percent power (high) for 15 seconds, or until just melted. Remove from the microwave. Whisk in the hot sauce and orange zest. Spoon over the fish.

5.18 Spice-Baked Trout Fillets

Servings: 4 persons

Preparation time: 8 minutes

Cooking Time: 8 minutes

Nutritional information: (Per Serving): Calories 172, Total Fat 7.5 g, Carbohydrates 1 g, Protein 23 g

Ingredients:

- 4 trout fillets (about 4 ounces each), rinsed and patted dry
- 1 tablespoon canola or corn oil
- 1 teaspoon smoked paprika
- ¾ teaspoon sugar
- ½ teaspoon ground cumin
- ¼ teaspoon salt
- 1/8 teaspoon ground allspice
- 1/8 teaspoon ground cinnamon
- Dash of cayenne

Directions:

- Heat the oven to 450°F. Line a baking sheet with aluminum foil. Lightly spray the foil with cooking oil spray.
- Place the fish on the baking sheet. Brush the top of the fish with the oil.
- In a small bowl, stir together the remaining ingredients. Sprinkle over the top of the fish.
- Bake for 8 minutes, or till the fish flakes easily when tested with a fork.

5.19 Tuna with Ginger Bok Choy

Servings: 4 persons

Preparation time: 10 to 12 minutes

Cooking Time: 10 minutes

Nutritional information: (Per Serving): Calories 186, Total Fat 5.5 g, Carbohydrates 5 g, Protein 30 g

Ingredients:

- 2 tuna steaks (about 8 ounces each), cut about ½ inch thick, rinsed and patted dry, halved
- 1/8 teaspoon salt
- 1/8 teaspoon pepper
- 1 teaspoon canola or corn oil and 1 teaspoon canola or corn oil, divided use
- 2 teaspoons minced peeled gingerroot
- ½ teaspoon bottled minced garlic or 1 medium garlic clove, minced
- 1 small head of bok choy or ½ medium head of napa cabbage, thinly sliced (about 8 cups)
- 2 teaspoons soy sauce (lowest sodium available)
- 1¼ teaspoons toasted sesame oil

Directions:

- Sprinkle both sides of the fish with salt and pepper. Using your fingertips, gently press the seasonings, so they adhere to the fish.
- In a large nonstick pan, heat 1 teaspoon canola oil over high heat, swirling to coat the bottom. Cook the fish for 2 minutes on each side or to the desired doneness. Transfer to a plate. Cover to keep warm.
- In the same skillet, heat the remaining 1 teaspoon canola oil, swirling to coat the bottom. Cook the gingerroot and garlic for 30 seconds, or until fragrant, stirring constantly.
- Stir in the bok choy. Cook for 3 minutes, or until just wilted, stirring occasionally.
- Stir in the soy sauce. Spoon the bok choy onto plates. Top with the fish. Drizzle with the sesame oil

5.20 Pan-Seared Tuna with Mandarin Orange Pico de Gallo

Servings: 4 persons

Preparation time: 10 minutes

Cooking Time: 10 minutes

Nutritional information: (Per Serving): Calories 185, Total Fat 3.0 g, Carbohydrates 11 g, Protein 28 g

Ingredients:

- ½ cup chopped red or yellow onion
- ½ teaspoon bottled minced garlic or 1 medium garlic clove, minced
- 1 tablespoon balsamic vinegar or red wine vinegar
- 1 teaspoon firmly packed light brown sugar

- 1/8 to ¼ teaspoon crushed red pepper flakes
- 1 11-ounce can mandarin oranges in juice, drained
- 1/3 cup chopped tomato
- 1/3 cup chopped avocado
- 1 Tablespoon Fresh Lime Juice
- 2 tuna steaks (about 8 ounces each), rinsed and patted dry

Directions:

- Lightly spray a medium saucepan with cooking oil spray. Brown the onion and garlic over high heat for 3 minutes, or till the onion is soft, stirring frequently.
- Stir in the vinegar, brown sugar, and red pepper flakes. Cook for 2 to 3 minutes, or till the brown sugar is dissolved, stirring frequently. Remove from the heat.
- Stir in the remaining pico de gallo ingredients. Put aside.
- Meanwhile, lightly spray a large pan with cooking oil spray. Heat over medium-high heat. Cook the fish for 5 minutes on each side or to the desired doneness. Cut each piece in half. Serve with the pico de gallo.

5.21 Tuna-Noodle Casserole

Servings: 4 persons

Preparation time: 10 minutes

Cooking Time: 40 minutes

Nutritional information: (Per Serving): Calories 216, Total Fat 2.5 g, Carbohydrates 29 g, Protein 22 g

Ingredients:

- 1 10¾-ounce can low-fat condensed cream of chicken soup (lowest sodium available)
- 1 cup fat-free milk
- 2 5-ounce cans of very low sodium white albacore tuna, packed in water, drained and flaked
- 10 ounces frozen mixed vegetables, such as peas, carrots, corn, and green beans, slightly thawed if needed to separate
- 3 ounces medium dried no-yolk noodles (about 2 cups), broken into small pieces
- ½ cup chopped onion
- 1 medium rib of celery, chopped
- ¼ cup snipped fresh parsley (optional)
- ¼ teaspoon paprika
- 1/8 teaspoon salt
- 1/8 teaspoon pepper

Directions:

- Heat the oven to 375°F.
- In a 2-quart glass casserole dish or 9-inch square glass baking dish, whisk together the soup and milk. Stir in the remaining ingredients.
- Bake, covered, for 25 minutes. Stir. Bake, covered, for 15 minutes, or till the noodles are tender.

5.22 Tuna-Topped Barley with Kalamata-Basil Tomatoes

Servings: 4 persons

Preparation time: 10 to 12 minutes

Cooking Time: 16 minutes

Nutritional information: (Per Serving): Calories 255, Total Fat 9.0 g, Carbohydrates 32 g, Protein 16 g

Ingredients:

- 1 cup uncooked quick-cooking barley
- 1½ ounces coarsely chopped spinach (about 1½ cups packed)
- 1 teaspoon bottled minced garlic or 2 medium garlic cloves, minced
- 1 tablespoon olive oil
- 1 cup grape tomatoes, quartered
- 15 kalamata olives, coarsely chopped
- ¼ cup chopped fresh basil (about 2/3 ounce) or 1 tablespoon dried, crumbled
- 1 6-ounce can very low sodium white albacore tuna, packed in water, drained, and flaked

Directions:

- Prepare the barley using the package directions, omitting the salt. Drain well in a colander. Transfer the barley to a large shallow dish.
- Add the spinach and garlic, tossing with tongs for 30 seconds, or till the spinach is slightly wilted. Cover to keep warm. Put aside.
- In a nonstick pan, heat the oil over medium-high heat, swirling to coat the bottom. Cook the tomatoes, olives, and basil for 2 minutes, or till the tomatoes are soft, stirring frequently. (Cooking this mixture just before layering all the ingredients helps keep the flavors "bright.")
- Sprinkle the tuna over the barley mixture. Top with the tomato mixture. (The heat from the barley and tomato layers will slightly warm the tuna.)

5.23 Dilled Albacore Cakes

Servings: 4 persons

Preparation time: 12 to 15 minutes

Cooking Time: 15 minutes

Nutritional information: (Per Serving): Calories 126, Total Fat 5.0 g, Carbohydrates 5 g, Protein 16 g

Ingredients:

- 2 5-ounce cans of very low sodium white albacore tuna, packed in water, drained and flaked
- ½ cup egg substitute
- ¼ cup plain dry breadcrumbs (lowest sodium available)
- ¼ cup shredded or grated Parmesan cheese
- 2 medium green onions, sliced
- 1 tablespoon snipped fresh dill weed or ½ teaspoon dried, crumbled
- ½ teaspoon pepper (coarsely ground preferred)
- 1/3 cup light mayonnaise
- ½ teaspoon grated lemon zest
- Sprigs of fresh dill weed (optional)

Directions:

- Heat the oven to 450°F. Lightly spray a medium shallow baking pan with cooking oil spray. Put aside.
- In a bowl, stir together the tuna, egg substitute, breadcrumbs, Parmesan, green onions, 1 tablespoon dill weed, and pepper. Shape into 6 patties. Arrange in a single layer in the baking pan.
- Bake on one side for 15 minutes or until lightly browned. Transfer to plates.
- Meanwhile, in a small bowl, stir together the mayonnaise and lemon zest.
- Spoon a dollop of the mayonnaise mixture onto each cake. Garnish with sprigs of dill weed.

5.24 Mussels in Creamy Wine Sauce

Servings: 4 persons

Preparation time: 5 minutes

Cooking Time: 15 minutes

Nutritional information: (Per Serving): Calories 151, Total Fat 3.0, Carbohydrates 11 g, Protein 14

Ingredients:

- 4 medium green onions, sliced
- ½ cup dry white wine (regular or nonalcoholic)
- ¼ teaspoon pepper
- 24 fresh debearded and rinsed medium mussels
- ½ cup fat-free evaporated milk
- 2 tablespoons Dijon mustard (lowest sodium available)
- 1½ teaspoons all-purpose flour

Directions:

- In a Dutch oven, bring the green onions, wine, and pepper to a boil over high heat. Add the mussels. Cook, covered, for 3 to 5 minutes, or till the mussels have opened. Turn off the heat. Leaving the cooking liquid in the pot, transfer the mussels to a serving dish, discarding any mussels that did not open during cooking.

- In a small bowl, whisk the milk, mustard, and flour. Whisk into the cooking liquid. Cook, still over high heat, for 5 minutes, or till the mixture is thickened to the desired consistency, whisking constantly. Pour over the mussels, stirring gently to coat.

5.25 Lemon-Garlic Scallops

Servings: 4 persons
Preparation time: 10 minutes
Cooking Time: 7 minutes
Nutritional information: (Per Serving): Calories 132, Total Fat 3.0 g, Carbohydrates 6 g, Protein 19 g

Ingredients:
- 2 tablespoons fresh lemon juice
- 1 tablespoon bottled minced garlic or 6 medium garlic cloves, minced
- 2 teaspoons olive oil
- 1/8 teaspoon pepper
- 1 pound sea scallops, rinsed and patted dry
- ½ medium red bell pepper, cut into 2 × 1/8-inch strips
- ¼ cup sliced green onions

Directions:
- In a large shallow dish, whisk together the lemon juice, garlic, oil, and pepper. Add the scallops, turning to coat. Cover and refrigerate for 10 minutes, turning the scallops once halfway through.
- Preheat a large nonstick skillet over medium-high heat. Cook the scallops with the marinade, bell pepper, and green onions for 4 to 6 minutes, or till the scallops are white on the outside and opaque almost to the center, and the sauce is bubbly. Turn the scallops once halfway through and stir the bell pepper and green onions occasionally. Don't overcook, or the scallops will be dry and rubbery.

5.26 Sherried Seafood Sauté

Servings: 4 persons
Preparation time: 10 minutes
Cooking Time: 7 minutes
Nutritional information: (Per Serving): Calories 119, Total Fat 2.0 g, Carbohydrates 4 g, Protein 19 g

Ingredients:
- 1 tablespoon light tub margarine
- 8 ounces peeled raw medium shrimp, rinsed and patted dry
- ½ cup pre-shredded carrot
- 3 medium green onions, sliced
- 1 teaspoon bottled minced garlic or 2 medium garlic cloves, minced
- 6 ounces lump crabmeat, flaked
- 2 tablespoons dry sherry or dry white wine (regular or nonalcoholic)

Directions:
- Lightly spray a large pan with cooking oil spray. Melt the margarine over medium-high heat, swirling to coat the bottom. Cook the shrimp, carrot, green onions, and garlic for 3 minutes, or till the shrimp are pink on the outside, stirring frequently.
- Stir in the crabmeat and sherry. Cook for 2 to

3 minutes, or until heated through, stirring constantly

5.27 Speedy Shrimp and Pasta

Servings: 4 persons

Preparation time: 5 minutes

Cooking Time: 8 minutes

Nutritional information: (Per Serving): Calories 352, Total Fat 4.5 g, Carbohydrates 17 g, Protein 30 g

Ingredients:

- 1-pound frozen peeled raw medium shrimp
- 14 to 16 ounces frozen vegetables, any combination (stir-fry mixture preferred)
- 9 ounces uncooked fresh fettuccine (lowest sodium available), halved crosswise and strands separated
- ½ cup water (plus more as needed)
- ¼ cup shredded or grated Parmesan or Romano cheese
- ¼ cup snipped fresh basil (about 2/3 ounce) or parsley
- Crushed red pepper flakes to taste (optional)

Directions:

- In a large skillet, stir together the shrimp, vegetables, pasta, and water. Bring to a boil over high heat, stirring occasionally. Reduce the heat to medium and cook, covered, for 3 minutes, stirring occasionally and adding more water if needed to keep the pasta from sticking to the bottom of the pan. Cook, still covered, for 1 to 3 minutes, or till the shrimp are pink on the outside, the vegetables are tender-crisp, and the pasta is tender.
- Serve sprinkled with Parmesan, basil, and red pepper flakes.

Chapter 6 Poultry

Protein-dense foods such as meat & poultry are readily available. They also include a variety of other minerals that your body needs, such as iodine, iron, magnesium, vitamins (particularly B12), and vital fatty acids. As a result, eating meat and poultry at least once a week as part of a well-balanced diet is a smart idea. However, the ideal option is to stay with uncooked, lean cuts of meat and to consume just the suggested serving size ideal option is to stay with uncooked, lean cuts of meat and to consume just the suggested serving size to avoid consuming too much sodium and fat intake. It contains iodine, which helps your body generate thyroid hormone; iron, which helps your body transport oxygen throughout your body; zinc, which helps your immune system stay strong, and your skin healthy, and it contains vitamins B12 and E, which help your nervous system and omega 3 fatty acids, which help your heart and brain stay healthy.

6.1 Marinated Hoisin Chicken

Servings: 4 persons

Preparation time: 6 minutes

Cooking Time: 50 minutes

Nutritional information: (Per Serving): Calories 154, Total Fat 4.5 g, Carbohydrates 3 g, Protein 25 g

Ingredients:

- ¼ cup hoisin sauce
- ¼ cup plain rice vinegar or cider vinegar
- tablespoons sesame seeds, dry-roasted
- 1¼ pounds skinless chicken breast halves with bone, all visible fat discarded

Directions:

- In a shallow glass dish, stir together the hoisin sauce, vinegar, and sesame seeds. Add the chicken, turning to coat. Cover and refrigerate for 1 to 24 hours, turning occasionally.
- About an hour before serving time, Heat the oven to 375°F.
- Arrange the chicken in a single layer in an 8-inch square glass baking dish, discarding the marinade.
- Bake for 45 to 55 minutes, or till the chicken is no longer pink in the center.

6.2 Baked Chicken with Winter Vegetables

Servings: 4 persons

Preparation time: 15 minutes

Cooking Time: 1 hour 15 minutes to 1 hour 30 minutes

Nutritional information: (Per Serving): Calories 313, Total Fat 3.5 g, Carbohydrates 30 g, Protein 29 g

Ingredients:

- skinless chicken breast halves with bone (7 to 8 ounces each), all visible fat discarded
- 8 small red potatoes, halved
- large carrots, cut into 1-inch pieces
- 1 small acorn squash, quartered, seeds and strings discarded
- 1 medium onion or fennel bulb, cut into 8 wedges
- ¼ cup water

- ¼ teaspoon dried thyme, crumbled
- 1/8 teaspoon salt
- ¼ teaspoon pepper
- 1 cup bottled chicken gravy (lowest sodium available)

Directions:

- Heat the oven to 375°F.
- Put the chicken in a 13 × 9 × 2-inch glass baking dish or a 3-quart glass casserole dish. Place the potatoes, carrots, squash, and onion around the chicken. Pour the water overall. Sprinkle with thyme, salt, and pepper.
- Bake, covered, for 1 hour 15 minutes to 1 hour 30 minutes, or till the chicken is no longer pink in the center, and the vegetables are tender. Transfer the chicken to a cutting board. Cut each breast in half, discarding the bones.
- Shortly before serving time, using the directions on the bottle, heat the gravy. Spoon over the cooked chicken and vegetables.

6.3 Chicken-and-Clementine Kebabs with Peach Glaze

Servings: 4 persons

Preparation time: 15 minutes

Cooking Time: 10 minutes

Nutritional information: (Per Serving): Calories 214, Total Fat 3.0 g, Carbohydrates 21 g, Protein 25 g

Ingredients:

- 1-pound boneless, skinless chicken breasts, all visible fat discarded, cut into 16 cubes
- Clementine, unpeeled, each cut into 8 wedges, seeds, if any, discarded
- 1 large red onion, cut into 16 wedges
- 1 medium yellow bell pepper, cut into 16 squares
- ¼ teaspoon salt
- ¼ teaspoon pepper
- ¼ cup all-fruit peach spread
- tablespoons fresh orange juice

Directions:

- Soak eight 10-inch wooden skewers in cold water for at least 10 minutes to keep them from charring or use metal skewers.
- Meanwhile, preheat the broiler. Lightly spray a broiler pan and rack with cooking oil spray. Put aside.
- For each kebab, skewer in any order two of the chicken cubes, clementine wedges, onion wedges, and bell pepper squares. Sprinkle the kebabs on all sides with salt and pepper.
- Broil the kebabs at least 4 inches from the heat for 8 minutes, turning once halfway through. Remove the broiler pan from the oven.
- Meanwhile, in a small bowl, whisk the all-fruit spread and orange juice. Spoon 2 tablespoons of the mixture into a small dish and reserve for drizzling.
- Brush the kebabs with the all-fruit spread mixture from the small bowl. Broil for 2 minutes, or till the chicken is no longer pink in the center. Drizzle with the reserved 2 tablespoons all-fruit spread mixture.

6.4 Baked Chicken with Crunchy Basil-Parmesan Pesto

Servings: 4 persons

Preparation time: 20 minutes

Cooking Time: 20 to 30 minutes

Nutritional information: (Per Serving): Calories 167, Total Fat 5.0 g, Carbohydrates 4 g, Protein 25 g

Ingredients:

- PESTO
- 1 cup firmly packed fresh basil (about 3 ounces)
- ½ cup firmly packed fresh Italian (flat-leaf) parsley
- ½ cup shredded or grated Parmesan cheese

- ¼ cup walnuts
- 1 teaspoon bottled minced garlic or 2 medium garlic cloves, minced
- tablespoons olive oil (extra-virgin preferred)
- tablespoons fat-free, low-sodium chicken broth
- CHICKEN
- 1½ pounds boneless, skinless chicken breast halves, all visible fat discarded
- ¼ cup cornflake crumbs
- 1 large lemon or 2 medium limes, each cut into 6 wedges (optional)

Directions:

- Heat the oven to 375°F.
- In a food processor or blender, process the basil, parsley, Parmesan, walnuts, and garlic to a paste, scraping the side as needed.
- With the processor running, gradually add the oil and broth. Process until smooth. Transfer 3 tablespoons of the pesto to a small bowl. Transfer the remaining pesto to a small airtight container and refrigerate for another use.
- Put the chicken in a shallow baking pan large enough to hold it in a single layer. Lightly brush the top with 3 tablespoons pesto. Sprinkle with the cornflake crumbs.
- Bake for 20 to 30 minutes, or till the chicken is no longer pink in the center. Serve with lemon wedges for squeezing over the chicken.

6.5 Chinese-Style Chicken

Servings: 4 persons

Preparation time: 10 minutes

Cooking Time: 30 minutes

Nutritional information: (Per Serving): Calories 158, Total Fat 4.0 g, Carbohydrates 4 g, Protein 25 g

Ingredients:

- 4 boneless, skinless chicken breast halves (about 4 ounces each), all visible fat discarded
- tablespoons soy sauce (lowest sodium available)
- tablespoons plain rice vinegar or cider vinegar
- tablespoons dry sherry or fresh orange juice
- 1 teaspoon toasted sesame oil
- 1 teaspoon honey
- ½ teaspoon bottled minced garlic or 1 medium garlic clove, minced
- 1 teaspoon cornstarch
- 1 tablespoon fresh orange juice or water

Directions:

- Heat the oven to 350°F.
- Arrange the chicken in a single layer in an 8-inch square baking dish.
- In a small bowl, stir together the soy sauce, vinegar, sherry, sesame oil, honey, and garlic. Pour over the chicken.
- Bake for 25 to 30 minutes, or till the chicken is no longer pink in the center. Transfer the chicken to a large plate. Cover to keep warm. Pour the sauce into a small saucepan.
- Put the cornstarch in a small bowl. Add the orange juice, whisking it to dissolve. Pour into the sauce. Cook over medium heat for 5 minutes, or until thickened and bubbly, whisking constantly. Spoon over the chicken.

6.6 Grilled Chicken with Strawberry-Fig Sauce

Servings: 4 persons

Preparation time: 20 minutes

Cooking Time: 15 minutes

Nutritional information: (Per Serving): Calories 223, Total Fat 3.5 g, Carbohydrates 23 g, Protein 26 g

Ingredients:

- 1 teaspoon paprika
- 1 teaspoon ground cumin
- ½ teaspoon ground ginger
- ¼ teaspoon pepper
- 1 tablespoon fresh lemon juice

- 1-pound boneless, skinless chicken breast halves, all visible fat discarded
- ½ cup chopped dried figs
- ½ cup fat-free, low-sodium chicken broth
- 1 medium shallot, sliced
- ¼ cup fresh orange juice
- 1/8 teaspoon ground cinnamon
- 1 pint strawberries, hulled and coarsely chopped (about 2 cups)
- 1 tablespoon balsamic vinegar
- 1 tablespoon snipped fresh parsley

Directions:

- Preheat the grill to medium. Lightly spray the grill rack with cooking oil spray.
- In a small bowl, stir together the paprika, cumin, ginger, and pepper. Put aside.
- Put the lemon juice in a dish. Add the chicken, turning to coat. Sprinkle the paprika mixture over both sides of the chicken. Using your fingertips, gently press the mixture, so it adheres to the chicken.
- Grill the chicken for 12 to 15 minutes, or until no longer pink in the center, turning once halfway through.
- Meanwhile, in a skillet, stir together the figs, broth, shallot, orange juice, and cinnamon. Bring to a boil over medium-high heat. Boil for 6 minutes, or until most of the liquid is evaporated, stirring occasionally. Remove from the heat.
- Stir in the strawberries and vinegar. Let stand for 3 to 5 minutes, or until slightly cooled. Serve the sauce over the chicken. Sprinkle with parsley.

6.7 Skillet Chicken with Dried Berries

Servings: 4 persons

Preparation time: 5 minutes

Cooking Time: 16 minutes

Nutritional information: (Per Serving): Calories 184, Total Fat 3.0 g, Carbohydrates 8 g, Protein 24 g

Ingredients:

- 4 boneless, skinless chicken breast halves (about 4 ounces each), all visible fat discarded
- 2/3 cup dry red wine (regular or nonalcoholic) or light cranberry juice cocktail
- ¼ cup sweetened dried cranberries, dried blueberries, dried cherries, or mixed dried fruit bits
- ½ teaspoon dried thyme, crumbled
- 1 teaspoon cornstarch
- 1 tablespoon water

Directions:

- Lightly spray a large skillet with cooking oil spray. Heat over medium-high heat. Cook the chicken for 1 minute on each side (the chicken won't be done at this point). Transfer to a large plate. Put aside.
- In the same skillet, stir together the wine, cranberries, and thyme. Increase the heat to high and bring it to a boil.
- Add the chicken, turning to coat. Reduce the heat and simmer, covered, for about 5 minutes, or till the chicken is no longer pink in the center. Transfer to a platter, leaving the sauce in the skillet. Cover to keep warm.
- Put the cornstarch in a small bowl. Add the water, whisking it to dissolve. Whisk into the sauce. Cook over medium heat for 5 minutes, or until thickened and bubbly, whisking constantly. Spoon over the chicken

6.8 Chicken with Fresh Fruit and Veggie Salsa

Servings: 4 persons

Preparation time: 10 minutes

Cooking Time: 10 minutes

Nutritional information: (Per Serving): Calories 150, Total Fat 3.0 g, Carbohydrates 5 g, Protein 25 g

Ingredients:

- ½ cup chopped fresh apricots, peaches, or nectarines
- 1 small tomato, chopped
- ¼ cup chopped red onion
- tablespoons fresh lemon juice
- ¼ teaspoon salt
- ¼ teaspoon finely grated peeled ginger root
- ¼ teaspoon bottled minced garlic or ½ medium garlic clove, minced

Directions:

- Preheat the grill to medium-high or preheat the broiler. Lightly spray the grill rack or the broiler pan and rack with cooking oil spray.
- In a bowl, stir together the salsa ingredients. Put aside.
- Grill the chicken or broil 4 to 5 inches from the heat for 5 minutes, or until lightly browned. Turnover. Grill or broil for 5 minutes, or until no longer pink in the center. Serve with salsa.

6.9 Lemony Chicken with Tarragon Oil

Servings: 4 persons

Preparation time: 8 minutes

Cooking Time: 8 minutes

Nutritional information: (Per Serving): Calories 192, Total fat 2.5 g, Carbohydrates 1 g, Protein 24 g

Ingredients:

- tablespoons olive oil (extra-virgin preferred)
- tablespoons fresh lemon juice
- ½ teaspoon dried tarragon, crumbled
- ¼ teaspoon pepper (coarsely ground preferred)
- ¼ teaspoon salt
- boneless, skinless chicken breast halves (about 4 ounces each), all visible fat discarded, flattened to the ½-inch thickness
- 1½ teaspoons salt-free grilling seasoning blend

Directions:

- If grilling, lightly sprays a grill rack with cooking oil spray. Preheat the grill to medium-high. If cooking on the stove, lightly spray a large skillet. Put aside.
- In a small bowl, whisk the oil, lemon juice, tarragon, pepper, and salt. Put aside.
- Sprinkle the chicken on both sides with the seasoning blend. Using your fingertips, gently press the seasonings, so they adhere to the chicken.
- If grilling, grill the chicken for 4 minutes. Turn over and grill for 2 to 4 minutes, or until no longer pink in the center. If using the stovetop, cook the chicken over high heat for 4 minutes. Turn over and cook for 2 minutes, or until no longer pink in the center. Transfer the chicken to a platter.
- Just before serving, whisk the oil mixture. Spoon over the chicken.

6.10 Cheesy Oven-Fried Chicken

Servings: 4 persons

Preparation time: s10 minutes

Cooking Time: 8 minutes

Nutritional information: (Per Serving): Calories 224, Total Fat 5.5 g, Carbohydrates 11 g, Protein 30 g

Ingredients:

- tablespoons fat-free milk
- 1 cup plain panko (Japanese breadcrumbs)
- ½ cup shredded or grated Parmesan cheese
- ½ to ¾ teaspoon dried basil, crumbled
- 1/8 teaspoon pepper
- 1- pound boneless, skinless chicken tenders, all visible fat discarded, cut into bite-size pieces

Directions:

Heat the oven to 450°F. Lightly spray a shallow baking pan with cooking oil spray.

Put the milk in a small shallow dish.

In a shallow dish, stir together the panko, Parmesan, basil, and pepper.

Put the dishes and baking pan in a row, assembly-line fashion. Dip several pieces of chicken in the milk, turning to coat and letting any excess drip off. Dip in the panko mixture, turning to coat and gently shaking off any excess. Transfer to the pan. Repeat with the remaining chicken, arranging the pieces in a single layer.

Bake for 7 to 9 minutes, or till the chicken is no longer pink in the center, and the crust begins to brow

6.11 Chicken with Leeks and Tomatoes

Servings: 4 persons

Preparation time: 12 minutes

Cooking Time: 18 to 22 minutes

Nutritional information: (Per Serving): Calories 177, Total Fat 5.5 g, Carbohydrates 6 g, Protein 25 g

Ingredients:

- 1-pound boneless, skinless chicken breast halves, all visible fat discarded, flattened to the ¼-inch thickness
- ¼ teaspoon pepper
- 1/8 teaspoon salt
- teaspoons olive oil
- 1 medium leek
- 1 cup halved red or yellow cherry tomatoes or a combination
- ¼ cup fat-free, low-sodium chicken broth
- 1 tablespoon snipped fresh sage, or 1 teaspoon dried sage
- 1 medium lemon, cut into 4 wedges

Directions:

- Sprinkle both sides of the chicken with pepper and salt. Using your fingertips, gently press the seasonings, so they adhere to the chicken.
- In a large nonstick pan, heat the oil over medium-high heat, swirling to coat the bottom. Put the chicken in the skillet. Reduce the heat to medium. Cook for 8 to 10 minutes, or till the chicken is no longer pink in the center, turning once halfway through. Transfer to a large plate. Cover to keep warm.
- Meanwhile, trim the leek, discarding all the green parts except a small amount of light green. Slice the light green part. Halve and slice the white part. (You should have about 1¼ cups total.) Put aside.
- After transferring the chicken to the plate, cook the leek in the same skillet over high heat for 3 minutes, stirring occasionally.
- Stir in the tomatoes. Cook for 2 minutes, stirring occasionally.
- Stir in the broth and bring it to a boil. Boil for 3 to 4 minutes, or until most of the liquid is evaporated.
- Stir in the sage. Spoon the sauce onto plates. Top with the chicken. Serve with the lemon wedges to squeeze over the chicken

6.12 Lemon-Pepper Chicken over Pasta

Servings: 4 persons

Preparation time: 15 minutes

Cooking Time: 20 minutes

Nutritional information: (Per Serving): Calories 259, Total Fat 4.5 g, Carbohydrates 25 g, Protein 29 g

Ingredients:

- 4 boneless, skinless chicken breast halves (about 4 ounces each), all visible fat discarded
- ½ medium lemon
- Pepper to taste
- 4 ounces dried spinach linguine or fettuccine
- 1 cup marinara sauce (lowest sodium available), at room temperature
- tablespoons snipped fresh basil or parsley

Directions:

- Heat the oven to 375°F.

- Arrange the chicken in a glass baking dish large enough to hold it in a single layer. Squeeze the lemon half over the chicken. Sprinkle generously with pepper. Using your fingertips, gently press the pepper, so it adheres to the chicken.
- Bake, covered, for 15 to 20 minutes, or till the chicken is no longer pink in the center. Cut the chicken into thick strips.
- Meanwhile, prepare the pasta using the package directions, omitting the salt. Drain well in a colander. Return the pan to the burner (turn off the heat) and return the pasta to the pan. Add the marinara sauce and basil, stirring to coat. Cover to keep warm.
- When the chicken is ready, spoon the pasta mixture onto plates. Top with the chicken

6.13 Coriander-Coated Chicken

Servings: 4 persons

Preparation time: 5 minutes

Cooking Time: 15 minutes

Nutritional information: (Per Serving): Calories 172, Total Fat 3.5 g, Carbohydrates 10 g, Protein 25 g

Ingredients:

- 4 boneless, skinless chicken breast halves (about 4 ounces each), all visible fat discarded
- tablespoons honey
- teaspoons ground coriander
- 1 to 2 teaspoons ground cumin
- 1 teaspoon sesame seeds, dry-roasted
- 1 teaspoon snipped fresh thyme or ¼ teaspoon dried, crumbled
- ¼ teaspoon salt
- ¼ to ½ teaspoon pepper (coarsely ground preferred

Directions:

- Heat the oven to 350°F.
- Lightly spray large ovenproof skillet with cooking oil spray. (If you don't have an ovenproof skillet, cook the chicken in a regular skillet and transfer it to a shallow baking pan.) Heat the skillet over medium-high heat. Cook the chicken for 1 minute on each side, or until browned (the chicken won't be done at this point). Remove from the heat, leaving the chicken in the skillet.
- Lightly brush the honey over the chicken.
- In a small bowl, stir together the remaining ingredients. Sprinkle over the chicken.
- Bake for 10 minutes, or till the chicken is no longer pink in the center

6.14 Spicy Peanut Chicken

Servings: 4 persons

Preparation time: 10 minutes

Cooking Time: 7 to 9 minutes

Nutritional information: (Per Serving): Calories 303, Total Fat 10.0 g, Carbohydrates 23 g, Protein 30 g

Ingredients:

- Cooking spray
- 1-pound boneless, skinless chicken breasts, all visible fat discarded, cut into bite-size pieces
- 1 medium green bell pepper, cut into bite-size pieces
- 10 ounces frozen brown rice
- ½ cupChunky Salsaor commercial salsa (lowest sodium available)
- 1 tablespoon peanut butter (lowest sodium available)

- 1 tablespoon soy sauce (lowest sodium available)
- 1 teaspoon bottled minced garlic or 2 medium garlic cloves, minced
- 1 teaspoon finely grated peeled ginger root
- ¼ cup coarsely chopped peanuts, dry-roasted
- ¼ cup snipped fresh basil (about 2/3 ounce)

Directions:

- Lightly spray a large skillet with cooking oil spray. Heat over medium-high heat. Cook the chicken and bell pepper for 3 to 5 minutes, or till the chicken are no longer pink in the center, stirring occasionally.
- Using the package directions, microwave the rice. Put aside.
- Meanwhile, stir the salsa, peanut butter, soy sauce, garlic, and ginger root into the chicken mixture. Cook for 3 minutes, or until thickened and bubbly, stirring constantly.
- Spoon the rice onto plates. Spoon the chicken mixture on top. Sprinkle with the peanuts and basil

6.15 Barbecue-Simmered Chicken Chunks

Servings: 4 persons

Preparation time: 4 minutes

Cooking Time: 6 minutes

Nutritional information: (Per Serving): Calories 199, Total Fat 3.0 g, Carbohydrates 17 g, Protein 24 g

Ingredients:

- Cooking spray
- 1-pound boneless, skinless chicken breasts, all visible fat discarded, cut into bite-size pieces
- ¼ cup barbecue sauce (lowest sodium available)
- ¼ cup all-fruit spread, such as red plum or apricot

Directions:

- Lightly spray a large skillet with cooking oil spray. Heat over medium-high heat. Cook the chicken for 3 minutes, stirring occasionally.
- Stir in the barbecue sauce and all-fruit spread. Cook for 3 minutes, or till the chicken is no longer pink in the center, and the sauce is heated through, stirring frequently.

6.16 Baked Dijon Chicken

Servings: 4 persons

Preparation time: 6 minutes

Cooking Time: 15 to 20 minutes

Nutritional information: (Per Serving): Calories 136, Total Fat 3.0 g, Carbohydrates 1 g, Protein 24 g

Ingredients:

- Cooking spray
- 4 boneless, skinless chicken breast halves (about 4 ounces each), all visible fat discarded
- 1 tablespoon Dijon or coarse-grain mustard (lowest sodium available)
- teaspoons fresh lemon or lime juice
- ½ teaspoon bottled minced garlic or 1 medium garlic clove, minced
- 1/8 teaspoon pepper

Directions:

- Heat the oven to 375°F. Lightly spray a 9-inch square glass baking dish with cooking oil spray.
- Arrange the chicken in a single layer of the dish.
- In a small bowl, stir together the remaining ingredients. Spread over the top of the chicken.
- Bake for 15 to 20 minutes, or till the chicken is no longer pink in the center

6.17 Poultry and Mango Stir-Fry

Servings: 4 persons

Preparation time: 6 minutes

Cooking Time: 10 to 12 minutes

Nutritional information: (Per Serving): Calories 203, Total Fat 6.5 g, Carbohydrates 10 g, Protein 26 g

Ingredients:

- Cooking spray
- 1-pound boneless, skinless chicken breasts, all visible fat discarded, cut into bite-size pieces
- tablespoons Asian-style stir-fry sauce (lowest sodium available)
- 1 cup coarsely chopped mango, drained and patted dry if bottled
- ¼ cup sliced almonds, dry-roasted

Directions:

- Lightly spray a large skillet with cooking oil spray. Heat over medium-high heat. Cook the chicken for 3 to 5 minutes, or until no longer pink in the center, stirring occasionally. Remove from the heat.
- Stir in the stir-fry sauce. Gently stir in the mango. Cook over medium heat for 5 minutes, or until heated through, stirring frequently. Serve sprinkled with the almond

6.18 Lemon-Sauced Chicken with Asparagus

Servings: 4 persons

Preparation time: 10 minutes

Cooking Time: 12 to 14 minutes

Nutritional information: (Per Serving): Calories 191, Total Fat 5.5 g, Carbohydrates 8 g, Protein 27 g

Ingredients:

- ½ cup fat-free, low-sodium chicken broth
- 1 teaspoon finely grated lemon zest
- tablespoons fresh lemon juice
- 1 tablespoon cornstarch
- 1 tablespoon soy sauce (lowest sodium available)
- 1 teaspoon sugar
- ¼ teaspoon pepper
- 1 teaspoon canola or corn oil and 1 teaspoon canola or corn oil, divided use
- 10 ounces frozen cut asparagus or broccoli florets, thawed and patted dry
- 1 small red bell pepper, cut into bite-size pieces
- 1-pound boneless, skinless chicken breasts, all visible fat discarded, cut into bite-size pieces

Directions:

- In a small bowl, whisk the sauce ingredients until the cornstarch is dissolved. Put aside.
- In a large skillet, heat 1 teaspoon oil over high heat, swirling to coat the bottom. Cook the asparagus and bell pepper for 1 minute, stirring constantly. Transfer to a large plate. Put aside.
- In the same skillet, heat the remaining 1 teaspoon oil over high heat, swirling to coat the bottom. Cook the chicken for 3 to 5 minutes, or until no longer pink in the center, stirring constantly. Make a well in the center.
- Stir the sauce. Pour into the well in the skillet. Cook for 4 minutes, or till the sauce is thickened and bubbly, stirring constantly.
- Return the asparagus mixture to the skillet, stirring to coat.

6.19 Light Chicken Chili

Servings: 4 persons

Preparation time: 8 minutes

Cooking Time: 15 to 18 minutes

Nutritional information: (Per Serving): Calories 227, Total Fat 2.0 g, Carbohydrates 26 g, Protein 25 g

Ingredients:

- Cooking spray
- 1-pound boneless, skinless chicken breasts, all visible fat discarded, cut into bite-size pieces
- 1 medium onion, chopped
- 1 teaspoon bottled minced garlic or 2 medium garlic cloves, minced

- cups fat-free, low-sodium chicken broth
- 1 4-ounce can chop green chiles, drained
- 1 teaspoon ground cumin
- ½ teaspoon pepper (white preferred)
- ¼ teaspoon salt
- 15.5-ounce cans no-salt-added navy or Great Northern beans, rinsed and drained, divided use.

Directions:

- Lightly spray a Dutch oven with cooking oil spray. Cook the chicken, onion, and garlic over high heat for 3 to 5 minutes, or till the chicken is no longer pink in the center, stirring occasionally.
- Stir in the remaining ingredients except for the beans. Bring to a boil. Reduce the heat and simmer for 5 minutes.
- Meanwhile, In a bowl, mash one can of the beans until smooth.
- When the chili has simmered, stir in the mashed beans and the remaining can of whole beans. Simmer for 5 minutes, or until heated through.

6.20 Chicken and Rice with Herbs

Servings: 4 persons

Preparation time: 5 minutes

Cooking Time: 30 minutes

Nutritional information: (Per Serving): Calories 320, Total Fat 5.5 g, Carbohydrates 33 g, Protein 29 g

Ingredients:

- teaspoons olive oil
- boneless, skinless chicken breast halves (about 4 ounces each), all visible fat discarded
- 1 large onion, chopped
- 1 teaspoon bottled minced garlic or 2 medium garlic cloves, minced
- 8 ounces pre-sliced button mushrooms
- 1 cup fat-free, low-sodium chicken broth
- ½ cup dry white wine (regular or nonalcoholic)
- ¼ teaspoon salt
- ¼ teaspoon dried thyme, crumbled
- 1/8 teaspoon dried basil, crumbled
- ¾ cup uncooked white rice

Directions:

- In a large nonstick pan, heat the oil over medium-high heat, swirling to coat the bottom. Cook the chicken for 2 minutes on each side, or until lightly browned (the chicken won't be done at this point). Transfer to a plate. Put aside.
- In the same skillet, stir together the onion and garlic. Cook over medium heat for 2 minutes. Stir in the mushrooms. Cook for 3 to 4 minutes, or till the onion is soft, stirring occasionally.
- Pour the broth and wine into the skillet, scraping to dislodge any browned bits. Stir in the salt, thyme, and basil. Increase the heat to medium-high and bring to a simmer.
- Stir in the rice. Top with the chicken. Return to a simmer. Reduce the heat and simmer, covered, for 15 to 20 minutes, or till the chicken is no longer pink in the center, and the rice is tender.

6.21 Plum Good Chicken

Servings: 4 persons

Preparation time: 15 minutes

Cooking Time: 50 minutes

Nutritional information: (Per Serving): Calories 419, Total Fat 11.0 g, Carbohydrates 48 g, Protein 33 g

Ingredients:

- 3-ounce packages of ramen noodles, seasoning packets discarded
- 16 ounces frozen Asian-style mixed vegetables
- 1¼ cups fat-free, low-sodium chicken broth

- boneless, skinless chicken breast halves (about 4 ounces each), all visible fat discarded
- ½ cup bottled Chinese plum sauce
- 1 teaspoon grated lemon zest
- 1 tablespoon fresh lemon juice
- 1 tablespoon grated peeled gingerroot
- 1 teaspoon soy sauce (lowest sodium available)

Directions:

- Heat the oven to 350°F.
- Break up the noodles over a 13 × 9 × 2-inch glass baking dish or a shallow 3-quart glass casserole dish. Spread them in a single layer. Spread the vegetables over the noodles. Pour the broth overall. Arrange the chicken on top.
- In a small bowl, stir together the remaining ingredients. Spoon over the chicken.
- Bake, covered, for 50 minutes, or till the chicken is no longer pink in the center, and the vegetables and noodles are tender.

6.22 Quick Cassoulet

Servings: 6 persons

Preparation time: 15 minutes

Cooking Time: 15 minutes

Nutritional information: (Per Serving): Calories 323, Total Fat 4.0 g, Carbohydrates 50 g, Protein 23 g

Ingredients:

- or 3 medium carrots, chopped
- medium ribs of celery, chopped
- 1 small onion, chopped
- 1 teaspoon bottled minced garlic or 2 medium garlic cloves, minced
- 8 ounces boneless, skinless chicken breasts, all visible fat discarded, cut into bite-size pieces
- 15.5-ounce cans no-salt-added Great Northern beans, rinsed and drained
- 1 8-ounce can no-salt-added tomato sauce
- 1 cup chopped lower-sodium, low-fat ham
- tablespoons firmly packed light or dark brown sugar
- tablespoons molasses (dark preferred)
- ¼ teaspoon ground allspice
- ¼ teaspoon dry mustard
- ¼ teaspoon pepper

Directions:

- Lightly spray a large skillet with cooking oil spray. Cook the carrots, celery, onion, and garlic over high heat for 7 minutes, or until tender, stirring frequently.
- Stir in the chicken. Cook for 2 to 3 minutes, or until just tender, stirring frequently.
- Stir in the remaining ingredients. Reduce the heat to medium-low. Cook for 5 minutes, or till the chicken is no longer pink in the center, and the cassoulet is heated through, stirring occasionally.

6.23 Chicken Jambalaya

Servings: 4 persons

Preparation time: 15 to 20 minutes

Cooking Time: 25 minutes

Nutritional information: (Per Serving): Calories 285, Total Fat 4.0 g, Carbohydrates 34 g, Protein 26 g

Ingredients:

- Cooking spray
- 1 medium green bell pepper, chopped
- 1 medium red bell pepper, chopped
- 1 medium rib of celery, chopped
- 1 medium onion, chopped
- 1½ teaspoons bottled minced garlic or 3 medium garlic cloves, minced
- 14.5-ounce cans no-salt-added diced tomatoes, undrained
- 1 cup uncooked instant brown rice
- 1 teaspoon dried thyme, crumbled
- 1 teaspoon pepper
- ¼ teaspoon salt
- ¼ teaspoon cayenne
- 12 ounces boneless, skinless chicken breasts,

- all visible fat discarded, cut into bite-size pieces
- ounces Canadian bacon, chopped

Directions:
- Lightly spray a Dutch oven with cooking oil spray. Cook the bell peppers, celery, onion, and garlic over high heat for 7 minutes, or until tender, stirring frequently.
- Stir in the tomatoes with liquid, rice, thyme, pepper, salt, and cayenne. Stir in the chicken and Canadian bacon. Increase the heat to high and bring it to a boil. Reduce the heat and simmer, covered, for 15 minutes, or till the chicken is no longer pink in the center, the rice is tender, and the liquid is absorbed.

6.24 Chicken Tenders in Creamy Herb Sauce

Servings: 4 persons

Preparation time: 10 minutes

Cooking Time: 15 minutes

Nutritional information: (Per Serving): Calories 173, Total Fat 5.0 g, Carbohydrates 3 g, Protein 27 g

Ingredients:
- teaspoons olive oil
- 1 pound chicken breast tenders, all visible fat discarded
- ½ cup fat-free plain Greek yogurt
- 1 teaspoon all-purpose flour
- 1/8 teaspoon salt
- 1/8 teaspoon cayenne
- ½ cup fat-free, low-sodium chicken broth
- 1 medium shallot, finely chopped
- ½ teaspoon bottled minced garlic or 1 medium garlic clove, minced
- ¼ cup snipped fresh parsley, oregano, dillweed, or another fresh herb

Directions:
- In a large nonstick pan, heat the oil over medium-high heat, swirling to coat the bottom. Cook the chicken for 4 minutes. Turnover. Cook for 2 to 3 minutes, or until no longer pink in the center. Transfer to a large plate. Cover to keep warm.
- Meanwhile, in a small bowl, whisk the yogurt, flour, salt, and cayenne. Put aside.
- In the same skillet, stir together the broth, shallot, and garlic. Bring to a boil, still over medium-high. Boil gently for about 5 minutes or until most of the liquid is evaporated.
- Reduce the heat to low. Whisk in the yogurt mixture and parsley. Cook for 1 minute, whisking constantly.
- Return the chicken to the skillet, stirring to coat it with the sauce.

6.25 Chicken with Broccoli and Bulgur

Servings: 4 persons

Preparation time: 10 minutes

Cooking Time: 15 minutes

Nutritional information: (Per Serving): Calories 210, Total Fat 3.0 g, Carbohydrates 25 g, Protein 23 g

Ingredients:
- 12 ounces boneless, skinless chicken breasts, all visible fat discarded, cut into bite-size pieces
- 1 teaspoon bottled minced garlic or 2 medium garlic cloves, minced
- 1½ cups water
- ¾ cup uncooked instant, or fine-grain, bulgur
- 1 teaspoon very low sodium chicken bouillon granules
- 1 teaspoon grated lemon zest
- ¼ teaspoon dried sage
- ¼ teaspoon salt
- 8 ounces broccoli florets, broken into bite-size pieces (about 3 cups)

- Pepper to taste (optional)

Directions:

- Lightly spray a large skillet with cooking oil spray. Heat over medium-high heat. Cook the chicken and garlic for 2 to 3 minutes, turning the chicken once halfway through.
- Stir in the water, bulgur, bouillon granules, lemon zest, sage, and salt. Arrange the broccoli on top. Increase the heat to high and bring it to a boil. Reduce the heat and simmer, covered, for 7 to 10 minutes, or till the chicken is no longer pink in the center, and the broccoli and bulgur are tender. Sprinkle with pepper.

6.26 Chicken and Black Bean Tacos

Servings: 6 persons

Preparation time: 10 minutes

Cooking Time: 10 minutes

Nutritional information: (Per Serving): Calories 221, Total Fat 3.0 g, Carbohydrates 27 g, Protein 22 g

Ingredients:

- 12 6-inch corn tortillas

For Filling

- 1 pound ground skinless chicken breast
- ½ cup chopped onion
- ½ teaspoon bottled minced garlic or 1 medium garlic clove, minced
- 1 15.5-ounce can no-salt-added black beans, undrained
- ¼ cup snipped fresh cilantro or parsley
- 1 tablespoon chili powder
- ½ teaspoon ground cumin
- ¼ teaspoon salt
- ¼ teaspoon pepper

For Toppings (Optional)

- ¼ cup chopped tomatoes
- ¼ cup shredded lettuce
- ¼ cup shredded low-fat Cheddar cheese
- ½ cup plus 2 tablespoonsChunky Salsaor commercial salsa

Directions:

- Heat the oven to 250°F. Wrap the tortillas in aluminum foil. Put in the oven while preparing the chicken mixture.
- In a large skillet, cook the chicken, onion, and garlic over high heat for 5 minutes, or till the chicken is no longer pink in the center, occasionally stirring to turn and break up the chicken.
- Stir in the remaining filling ingredients. Cook for 5 minutes, or until heated through.
- Place 2 tortillas on each plate. Spoon the chicken mixture over half of each tortilla. Add the toppings. Fold the other half of each tortilla over the filling.

6.27 Grilled Chicken Burgers

Servings: 4 persons

Preparation time: 8 to 10 minutes

Cooking Time: 8 to 10 minutes

Nutritional information: (Per Serving): Calories 136, Total Fat 2.5 g, Carbohydrates 10 g, Protein 17 g

Ingredients:

- Cooking spray
- 1 pound ground skinless chicken breast
- ½ cup plain dry breadcrumbs (lowest sodium available)
- medium green onions, chopped
- tablespoons barbecue sauce (lowest sodium available)
- 1 tablespoon fresh lemon juice
- teaspoons Worcestershire sauce (lowest sodium available)
- 1/8teaspoon salt

Directions:

- Lightly spray the grill rack or the broiler pan

and rack with cooking oil spray. Preheat the grill to medium-high or preheat the broiler.

- In a large bowl, using your hands or a spoon, combine all the burger ingredients. Shape into 6 patties about ¼ inch thick.
- Grill the patties or broil 3 to 4 inches from the heat for 4 to 5 minutes on each side, or till the patties are no longer pink in the center.

6.28 Cornmeal Chicken Muffinwiches

Servings: 4 persons

Preparation time: 10 to 12 minutes

Cooking Time: 15 to 20 minutes

Nutritional information: (Per Serving): Calories 230, Total Fat 4.5 g, Carbohydrates 31 g, Protein 16 g

Ingredients:

- Cooking spray
- 1 8.5-ounce package corn muffin mix
- large egg whites
- 1/3 cup fat-free milk
- 8 ounces coarsely chopped cooked skinless chicken breast (about 2 cups), cooked without salt, all visible fat discarded
- medium green onions, sliced
- ¼ teaspoon dried sage

Directions:

- Heat the oven to 450°F. Lightly spray a standard 6-cup muffin pan with cooking oil spray or line it with paper bake cups. Put aside.
- Prepare the muffin mix using the package directions, substituting the egg whites for the egg and the fat-free milk for whole milk. Fold in the chicken, green onions, and sage. Spoon into the muffin cups.
- Bake for 15 to 20 minutes, or until a wooden toothpick inserted in the center comes out clean. Transfer the muffins from the muffin pan to a cooling rack. Serve warm or at room temperature. Freeze any extra muffins in an airtight bag for up to two months.

6.29 Turkey Tenderloin with Cranberry-Jalapeño Sauce

Servings: 4 persons

Preparation time: 10 to 12 minutes

Cooking Time: 32 to 42 minutes

Nutritional information: (Per serving) Calories 280, Total Fat 2.0 g, Carbohydrates 37 g, Protein 28 g

Ingredients:

- Cooking spray
- 1 1-pound turkey tenderloin
- 1 teaspoon canola or corn oil
- 14 ounces whole-berry cranberry sauce
- teaspoons grated orange zest
- 1½ tablespoons snipped fresh cilantro
- 1 teaspoon minced fresh jalapeño

Directions:

- Heat the oven to 450°F.
- Lightly spray large glass baking dish with cooking oil spray. Put the turkey in the baking dish, tucking the ends of the turkey under for even cooking. Brush the top with the oil.
- Roast for 20 minutes.
- Meanwhile, in a small saucepan, stir together the cranberry sauce, orange zest, cilantro, and jalapeño. Cook over low heat for 5 minutes, or until heated through, stirring once. Remove from the heat. Spoon 1 cup of the sauce into a small bowl and put it aside. You should have about ½ cup of sauce left in the pan.
- Turn the turkey over. Baste with about half the cranberry sauce from the pan.
- Roast for 10 to 20 minutes, or till the turkey registers 160°F on an instant-read thermometer, basting once about halfway through with the remaining sauce in the pan. Transfer the turkey to a cutting board. Let stand for 5 to 10 minutes, or until it is no

longer pink in the center and registers 165°F. Thinly slice diagonally across the grain. Serve with the reserved 1 cup sauce spooned on top

6.30 Southwestern Turkey Stew

Servings: 8 persons

Preparation time: 12 to 15 minutes

Cooking Time: 28 minutes

Nutritional information: (Per Serving): Calories 185, Total Fat 1.0 g, Carbohydrates 20 g, Protein 24 g

Ingredients:

- ¼ cup all-purpose flour
- ½ teaspoon salt
- 1/8 teaspoon pepper
- 1½ pounds turkey tenderloins, cut into ½-inch cubes
- 14.5-ounce cans no-salt-added diced tomatoes, undrained
- 1¼ cups fat-free, low-sodium chicken broth
- 10 ounces frozen whole-kernel corn
- 1 large onion, chopped
- 1 4-ounce can chop green chiles, drained
- teaspoons bottled minced garlic or 4 medium garlic cloves, minced
- 1½ teaspoons ground cumin
- 1½ teaspoons dried oregano, crumbled
- ¼ cup snipped fresh cilantro

Directions:

- In a large shallow dish, stir together the flour, salt, and pepper. Add the turkey, turning to coat well and gently shaking off any excess. Transfer to a Dutch oven.
- Stir in the remaining ingredients except for the cilantro. Bring to a boil over high heat. Reduce the heat and simmer, covered, for 25 minutes, or till the turkey is no longer pink in the center, stirring occasionally. Just before serving, stir in the cilantro.

6.31 Roast Turkey Tenderloin with Mashed Sweet Potatoes and Fruit

Servings: 8 persons

Preparation time: 15 minutes

Cooking Time: 35 to 40 minutes

Nutritional information: (Per Serving): Calories 240, Total Fat 1.5 g, Carbohydrates 27 g, Protein 29 g

Ingredients:

- Cooking spray
- pounds turkey tenderloins
- ½ teaspoon ground coriander
- ¼ teaspoon pepper and 1/8 teaspoon pepper, divided use
- 1/8 teaspoon salt and 1/8 teaspoon salt, divided use
- pounds sweet potatoes, peeled and cut into large chunks
- medium pears (Bartlett or Bosc preferred) or apples (Golden Delicious, Granny Smith, or Rome Beauty preferred), peeled and cut into large chunks
- 1 cinnamon stick (about 3 inches long)
- 1 tablespoon light tub margarine

Directions:

- Heat the oven to 350°F.
- Lightly spray large glass baking dish with cooking oil spray. Put the turkey in the baking dish, tucking the ends of the turkey under for even cooking. Sprinkle with the coriander, ¼ teaspoon pepper, and 1/8 teaspoon salt.
- Roast for 35 to 40 minutes, or till the turkey registers 160°F on an instant-read thermometer. Transfer the turkey to a cutting board. Let stand for 5 to 10 minutes, or until it is no longer pink in the center and registers 165°F. Thinly slice diagonally across the grain.
- Meanwhile, put the sweet potatoes, pears, and cinnamon stick in a Dutch oven. Add enough water to cover. Bring to a boil over high heat. Reduce the heat and simmer, covered, for 20

minutes, or till the sweet potatoes and peas are tender. Drain well. Discard the cinnamon stick.

- If using an electric hand mixer to beat the potato mixture, leave the mixture in the pan. If using an electric stand mixer, transfer the mixture to a large mixing bowl. Beat on low speed until smooth. Stir in the margarine, remaining 1/8 teaspoon pepper, and remaining 1/8 teaspoon salt. (You can use a potato masher if you prefer.) Serve the potato mixture with the turkey

6.32 Turkey Medallions with Rosemary-Mushroom Gravy

Servings: 4 persons

Preparation time: 10 to 12 minutes

Cooking Time: 21 minutes

Nutritional information: (Per Serving): Calories 182, Total Fat 3.0 g, Carbohydrates 7 g, Protein 30 g

Ingredients:

- 1 tablespoon cornstarch
- ½ cup fat-free, low-sodium chicken broth
- ¼ teaspoon salt
- 1/8 teaspoon pepper
- Cooking spray
- 1 teaspoon olive oil and 1 teaspoon olive oil, divided use
- 1 1-pound turkey tenderloin, all visible fat discarded, cut crosswise into ¼-inch slices
- tablespoons balsamic vinegar
- 1 teaspoon finely snipped fresh rosemary or ¼ teaspoon dried, crushed
- 8 ounces chanterelle or button mushrooms, sliced (about 2½ cups)
- ¼ cup chopped shallot or onion

Directions:

- Put the cornstarch in a small bowl. Add the broth, stirring to dissolve. Stir in the salt and pepper. Put aside.

- Lightly spray a large skillet with cooking oil spray. Heat 1 teaspoon oil over medium-high heat, swirling to coat the bottom. Cook half the turkey medallions in a single layer for 2 minutes on each side, or until no longer pink in the center. Transfer to a large plate. Cover to keep warm. Repeat with the remaining 1 teaspoon oil and remaining turkey medallions. Remove the skillet from the heat.
- Add the vinegar and rosemary to the skillet, scraping to dislodge any browned bits. Return to the heat. Stir in the mushrooms and shallot. Cook over medium heat for 5 minutes, or till the mushrooms are soft, stirring occasionally.
- Stir the cornstarch mixture. Pour into the mushroom mixture. Cook for 5 minutes, or until thickened and bubbly, stirring frequently. Serve the sauce with the turkey.

6.33 Turkey and Artichoke Fettuccine

Servings: 4 persons

Preparation time: 8 minutes

Cooking Time: 15 minutes

Nutritional information: (Per Serving): Calories 483, Total Fat 5.0 g, Carbohydrates 61 g, Protein 48 g

Ingredients:

- 8 ounces dried whole-grain fettuccine
- 9 ounces frozen artichoke hearts or frozen broccoli florets
- Cooking spray
- 1 pound turkey tenderloin, all visible fat discarded, cut into bite-size pieces
- ½ teaspoon bottled minced garlic or 1 medium garlic clove, minced
- 1 tablespoon all-purpose flour
- 1 12-ounce can fat-free evaporated milk
- ¼ teaspoon salt
- ¼ teaspoon dried marjoram or basil, crumbled
- 1/8 teaspoon pepper
- 1/8 teaspoon of ground nutmeg (optional)

- ½ cup shredded or grated Parmesan cheese

Directions:

- In a soup pot, prepare the pasta using the package directions, omitting the salt. During the last 5 minutes of cooking, stir in the artichokes. Drain well in a colander. Halve any large artichoke hearts. Return to the pan. Cover to keep warm.
- Meanwhile, lightly spray a large skillet with cooking oil spray. Heat over medium-high heat. Cook the turkey and garlic for 3 minutes, or till the turkey is no longer pink in the center, stirring occasionally.
- Stir in the flour. Stir in the remaining ingredients except for the Parmesan. Cook for 6 minutes, or until thickened and bubbly, stirring constantly.
- Add the turkey mixture and Parmesan to the pasta, tossing to coat.

6.34 Velvet Turkey and Herbs

Servings: 4 persons

Preparation time: 10 minutes

Cooking Time: 10 minutes

Nutritional information: (Per Serving): Calories 224, Total Fat 1.0 g, Carbohydrates 16 g, Protein 36 g

Ingredients:

- Cooking spray
- 1 pound turkey tenderloin, all visible fat discarded, cut into bite-size pieces
- ¼ cup chopped shallot or onion
- ½ teaspoon bottled minced garlic or 1 medium garlic clove, minced
- tablespoons all-purpose flour
- 1 12-ounce can fat-free evaporated milk
- 1 tablespoon snipped fresh oregano or ½ teaspoon dried, crumbled
- 1 tablespoon snipped fresh parsley
- 1 teaspoon snipped fresh basil or ¼ teaspoon dried, crumbled
- 1⁄8 teaspoon salt

Directions:

- Lightly spray a large skillet with cooking oil spray. Heat over medium-high heat. Cook the turkey, shallot, and garlic for 3 to 4 minutes, or till the turkey is no longer pink in the center, stirring occasionally.
- Stir in the flour. Stir in the remaining ingredients. Cook for 4 minutes, or until thickened and bubbly, stirring constantly.

6.35 Currant Turkey with Capers

Servings: 4 persons

Preparation time: 8 minutes

Cooking Time: 15 minutes

Nutritional information: (Per Serving): Calories 188, Total Fat 1.0 g, Carbohydrates 10 g, Protein 28 g

Ingredients:

- Cooking spray
- 1 pound turkey cutlets, all visible fat discarded
- ½ cup dry white wine and 2 tablespoons dry white wine (regular or nonalcoholic), divided use
- ¼ cup dried currants or raisins
- tablespoons chopped onion
- 1 tablespoon capers, drained and chopped
- ½ teaspoon bottled minced garlic or 1 medium garlic clove, minced
- ¼ teaspoon salt
- ¼ teaspoon ground cinnamon
- 1 tablespoon cornstarch

Directions:

- Lightly spray a large skillet with cooking oil spray. Heat over medium-high heat. Cook half the turkey for 1 minute on each side, or until browned (the turkey will not be done at this point). Transfer to a large plate. Repeat with the remaining turkey. Put aside.
- Slowly pour ½ cup wine into the skillet, scraping to dislodge any browned bits. Stir in the currants, onion, capers, garlic, salt, and cinnamon. Bring to a boil over medium-high heat. Return the turkey to the skillet. Reduce the heat and simmer, covered, for 2 minutes, or till the turkey is no longer pink in the center. Transfer the turkey to a separate large plate, leaving the sauce in the skillet. Cover the plate to keep it warm.
- Put the cornstarch in a small bowl. Add the remaining 2 tablespoons of wine, whisking to dissolve. Whisk into the wine mixture in the skillet. Cook for 5 minutes, or until thickened and bubbly, whisking constantly. Serve over the turkey.

6.36 Fresh Herb Turkey Loaf

Servings: 6 persons

Preparation time: 12 to 15 minutes

Cooking Time: 40 to 45 minutes

Nutritional information: (Per Serving): Calories 159, Total Fat 1.5 g, Carbohydrates 13 g, Protein 23 g

Ingredients:

- Cooking spray
- 1 pound ground skinless turkey breast
- 1 cup uncooked rolled oats
- ½ medium red bell pepper, chopped
- 1 small to medium rib of celery, finely chopped
- ¼ cup chopped shallot or onion
- large egg whites
- tablespoons snipped fresh Italian (flat-leaf) parsley and 1 teaspoon snipped fresh Italian (flat-leaf) parsley, divided use
- tablespoons snipped fresh basil or oregano, and 1 teaspoon snipped fresh basil or oregano, divided use
- ½ teaspoon salt
- ¼ teaspoon pepper
- ½ cup no-salt-added tomato sauce

Directions:

- Heat the oven to 350°F. Lightly spray a 9 × 5 × 3-inch loaf pan with cooking oil spray.
- In a bowl, using your hands or a spoon, combine the turkey, oats, bell pepper, celery, shallot, egg whites, 2 tablespoons parsley, 2 tablespoons basil, salt, and pepper. Transfer to the pan, lightly smoothing the top.
- Bake for 40 to 45 minutes, or till the loaf registers 165°F on an instant-read thermometer. Using paper towels, pat dries any moisture that has risen to the top. Let stand at room temperature for 5 minutes to finish cooking. Cut the loaf into 6 slices. Transfer to plates.
- Pour the tomato sauce into a small microwaveable bowl. Microwave, covered, on 100 percent power (high) for 40 to 45 seconds, or until hot. Pour over the turkey loaf slices. Sprinkle with the remaining 1 teaspoon parsley and the remaining 1 teaspoon basil.

Chapter 7 Meats

When it comes to nutrition, meat is a wonderful source of protein, vitamins, and minerals. However, if you are already consuming more than 100g of meat per day, it is recommended to reduce your intake to 80g per day instead. Depending on the kind of meat, some are rich in saturated fat, which may cause blood cholesterol levels to rise if consumed in excess. Making better choices may help you consume meat as one of a well-balanced diet as part of a healthy lifestyle. You should reduce your intake of red and frozen meat. A proper diet may contain protein from meat, fish, eggs, and non-animal resources such as soybeans and pulses, as well as protein from plant sources, including beans and pulses. Protein-dense meats like chicken, hog, lamb, and beef are available in plenty. Iron, zinc, and B vitamins are all found in large amounts in red meat. Beef is one of the most important dietary rich in vitamin B12 in the Western diet. When it comes to storing, preparing, and cooking meat, food cleanliness is critical.

7.1 Molasses-Marinated Tenderloin

Servings: 4 persons

Preparation time: 5 minutes

Cooking Time: 12 minutes

Nutritional information: (Per Serving): Calories 239, Total Fat 5.0 g, Carbohydrates 23 g, Protein 24 g

Ingredients:

- 1/3 cup light molasses
- 1 medium shallot, chopped
- 2 tablespoons balsamic vinegar or red wine vinegar
- ½ teaspoon dried thyme, crumbled
- ¼ teaspoon salt
- ¼ teaspoon pepper
- 1 1-pound beef tenderloin, all visible fat discarded

Directions:

- In a large shallow glass dish, stir together the molasses, shallot, vinegar, thyme, salt, and pepper. Add the beef, turning to coat. Cover and refrigerate for about 24 hours, turning occasionally.
- About 15 minutes before serving time, transfer the beef to a cutting board, reserving the marinade. Cut the beef crosswise into 4 slices.
- Heat a large nonstick skillet over medium-high heat. Cook the beef for 3 minutes. Turnover. Cook for 3 to 5 minutes or to the desired doneness. Transfer to a large plate. Cover to keep warm.
- Pour the marinade into the same skillet. Cook, still over medium-high heat, for 3 minutes, or till the marinade begins to boil. Spoon over the beef.

7.2 Beef Tenderloin on Herbed White Beans

Servings: 4 persons

Preparation time: 10 minutes

Cooking Time: 9 minutes

Nutritional information: (Per Serving): Calories 261, Total Fat 6.5 g, Carbohydrates 19 g, Protein 30 g

Ingredients:

- Pepper to taste
- 1 1-pound beef tenderloin, all visible fat discarded, cut crosswise into 4 slices

- Cooking spray
- 1 teaspoon olive oil
- ½ cup chopped red onion
- ½ teaspoon bottled minced garlic or 1 medium garlic clove, minced
- 1 15.5-ounce can no-salt-added navy beans, about 1 inch of liquid discarded
- 1 tablespoon chopped fresh herbs or 1 teaspoon dried herbs, crumbled, and (optional) fresh herbs for garnish, divided use
- ½ teaspoon salt

Directions:

- Sprinkle the pepper over both sides of the beef. Using your fingertips, gently press the pepper, so it adheres to the beef.
- Lightly spray a large skillet with cooking oil spray. Heat over medium-high heat. Cook the beef for 3 minutes. Turnover. Cook for 3 to 5 minutes or to the desired doneness.
- Meanwhile, lightly spray a small saucepan with cooking oil spray. Heat the oil over medium-high heat, swirling to coat the bottom. Brown the onions and garlic for 3 minutes, or till the onion is soft, stirring frequently.
- Stir in the beans with the remaining liquid, herbs, and salt. Reduce the heat to low. Cook for 5 minutes, or until heated through. Spoon onto plates. Top with the beef. Garnish with the remaining fresh herbs.

7.3 Flank Steak with Blueberry-Pomegranate Sauce

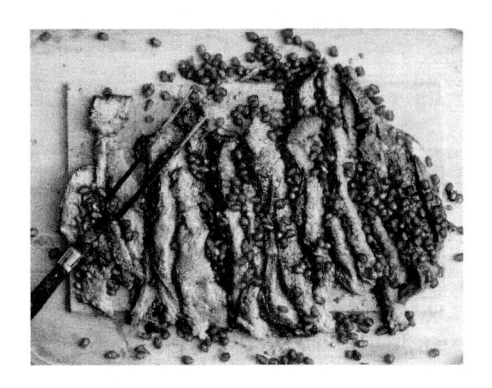

Servings: 4 persons

Preparation time: 10 minutes

Cooking Time: 25 minutes

Nutritional information: (Per Serving): Calories 185, Total Fat 6.5 g, Carbohydrates 6 g, Protein 24 g

Ingredients:

- ¼ teaspoon pepper
- ¼ teaspoon salt
- 1 1-pound flank steak, cut about ¾ inch thick, all visible fat discarded
- Cooking spray
- ½ cup fresh or frozen blueberries (wild preferred)
- ½ cup fat-free, no-salt-added beef broth
- ¼ cup frozen pomegranate juice concentrate (blueberry-pomegranate preferred) or grape juice concentrate, thawed
- ½ teaspoon bottled minced garlic or 1 medium garlic clove, minced
- 2 tablespoons snipped fresh parsley
- 1 tablespoon maple syrup (optional)
- 2 teaspoons balsamic vinegar

Directions:

- Sprinkle the pepper and salt over both sides of the beef. Using your fingertips, gently press the seasonings, so they adhere to the beef.
- Lightly spray a large skillet with cooking oil spray. Heat over medium heat. Cook the beef for 10 to 12 minutes, or until rare (the beef won't be done at this point), turning once halfway through. Transfer the beef to a cutting board.
- In the same skillet, stir together the blueberries, broth, pomegranate juice, and garlic, scraping the skillet to dislodge any browned bits. Bring to a boil over medium-high heat. Boil for 5 to 6 minutes, or till the liquid is reduced to about 1/3 cup.

- While the sauce boils, thinly slice the steak across the grain. Put aside.
- Stir the parsley, maple syrup, and vinegar into the sauce. Return the beef to the skillet, turning to coat it with the sauce. Cook for 1 to 2 minutes, or till the beef is heated through and cooked to the desired doneness.

7.4 Pepper-Rubbed Beef with Mushroom Sauce

Servings: 4 persons

Preparation time: 7 minutes

Cooking Time: 10 minutes

Nutritional information: (Per Serving): Calories 235, Total Fat 7.0 g, Carbohydrates 12 g, Protein 30 g

Ingredients:

- Cooking spray
- 2 teaspoons pepper (coarsely ground preferred)
- ¼ teaspoon salt
- 1 1-pound flank steak, all visible fat discarded
- ounces pre-sliced button mushrooms (about 1¼ cups)
- 2 medium green onions, sliced
- ½ teaspoon bottled minced garlic or 1 medium garlic clove, minced
- 1 tablespoon all-purpose flour
- 2 teaspoons Dijon mustard (lowest sodium available)
- 1 cup fat-free evaporated milk

Directions:

- Preheat the broiler. Lightly spray the broiler pan and rack with cooking oil spray. Put aside.
- Sprinkle the pepper and salt on both sides of the beef. Using your fingertips, gently press the seasonings, so they adhere to the beef.
- Broil about 4 inches from the heat for 3 to 5 minutes on each side or the desired doneness. Transfer to a cutting board. Thinly slice the beef diagonally across the grain.
- Meanwhile, lightly spray a medium saucepan with cooking oil spray. Cook the mushrooms, green onions, and garlic over medium heat for 5 mins, or till the mushrooms are just soft.
- Stir in the flour. Add the mustard. Pour in the milk all at once. Cook for 5 minutes, or until thickened to the desired consistency, stirring constantly. Spoon over the beef.

7.5 Grilled Sirloin Steak with Lemony Horseradish Sauce

Servings: 4 persons

Preparation time: 7 minutes

Cooking Time: 8 to 10 minutes

Nutritional information: (Per Serving): Calories 213, Total Fat 9.0 g, Carbohydrates 6 g, Protein 25 g

Ingredients:

- 1/3 cup fat-free sour cream
- 1/3 cup light mayonnaise
- 2 tablespoons bottled white horseradish, drained
- ½ teaspoon grated lemon zest
- 1 teaspoon fresh lemon juice
- 1-pound boneless top sirloin steak, all visible fat discarded, cut into 4 pieces

Directions:

- Lightly spray the grill rack with cooking oil spray. Preheat on medium-high.
- In a small bowl, whisk the sauce ingredients. Put aside or cover and refrigerate until serving time.
- Grill the beef for 4 to 5 minutes on each side or the desired doneness. Serve topped with the sauce.

7.6 Ginger Beef and Broccoli Stir-Fry

Servings: 4 persons

Preparation time: 15 minutes

Cooking Time: 15 minutes

Nutritional information: (Per Serving): Calories 214, Total Fat 7.5 g, Carbohydrates 8 g, Protein 29 g

Ingredients:

- 1/3 cup fat-free, low-sodium chicken broth
- 2 tablespoons soy sauce (lowest sodium available)
- 2 tablespoons water and 1 to 2 tablespoons water (as needed), divided use
- 2 teaspoons cornstarch
- 2 teaspoons grated peeled gingerroot
- ½ teaspoon bottled minced garlic or 1 medium garlic clove, minced
- ¼ teaspoon toasted sesame oil
- 1/8 teaspoon crushed red pepper flakes
- 1 teaspoon canola or corn oil and 1 teaspoon canola or corn oil, divided use
- 1-pound boneless top sirloin steak, all visible fat discarded, cut across the grain into ¼-inch strips
- ounces broccoli florets, broken into 1-inch pieces (about 4½ cups)
- 2 medium green onions, thinly sliced (optional)

Directions:

- In a small bowl, combine the broth, soy sauce, 2 tablespoons water, cornstarch, ginger root, garlic, sesame oil, and red pepper flakes, whisking until the cornstarch is dissolved. Put aside.
- In a large nonstick pan, heat 1 teaspoon canola oil over medium-high heat, swirling to coat the bottom. Cook half the beef for 2 to 3 minutes, or until browned, stirring and turning constantly. Transfer to a medium plate. Repeat with the remaining beef (no additional oil needed). Set all the beef aside.
- Heat the remaining 1 teaspoon canola oil in the same skillet, swirling to coat the bottom. Cook the broccoli for 2 to 3 minutes, or until tender-crisp, stirring frequently. If the mixture becomes too dry, add the remaining 1 to 2 tablespoons of water as needed.
- Stir the beef into the broccoli. Stir the broth mixture, then stir it into the broccoli. Cook for 1 to 2 minutes, or till the beef is heated through and the broth mixture is thickened. Sprinkle with green onions.

7.7 Sliced Sirloin with Leek Sauce

Servings: 4 persons

Preparation time: 10 minutes

Cooking Time: 25 minutes

Nutritional information: (Per Serving): Calories 171, Total Fat 4.5 g, Carbohydrates 4 g, Protein 24 g

Ingredients:

- Cooking spray
- 1 1-pound boneless top sirloin steak, about 1½ inches thick, all visible fat discarded
- ¾ cup water and 2 tablespoons water, divided to use
- ¼ cup dry red wine (regular or nonalcoholic)
- ½ cup sliced leeks (white and light green parts only)
- ½ teaspoon very low sodium beef bouillon granules
- ½ teaspoon bottled minced garlic or 1 medium garlic clove, minced
- ½ teaspoon salt
- 1 tablespoon plus 1 teaspoon of all-purpose flour

Directions:

- Lightly spray a large skillet with cooking oil

spray. Heat over medium-high heat. Cook the beef for 8 minutes on each side or to the desired doneness. Transfer to a plate. Cover to keep warm.

- In the same skillet, stir together ¾ cup water, the wine, leeks, bouillon granules, garlic, and salt. Bring to a simmer, still over medium-high. Reduce the heat and simmer, covered, for 3 minutes.
- Meanwhile, in a small bowl, whisk the flour and the remaining 2 tablespoons of water. Whisk into the sauce. Cook for 3 minutes, or till the desired consistency, whisking constantly.
- Cut the beef crosswise into ½-inch slices. Serve topped with the sauce.

7.8 Steak with Sun-Dried Tomatoes

Servings: 4 persons

Preparation time: 15 minutes

Cooking Time: 15 minutes

Nutritional information: (Per Serving): Calories 156, Total Fat 5.0 g, Carbohydrates 3 g, Protein 24 g

Ingredients:

- sun-dried tomatoes, packed in oil, drained, patted dry, and coarsely chopped
- ¼ to ½ cup pre-shredded carrot
- 1 medium green onion, sliced
- 2 teaspoons chopped fresh basil or ½ teaspoon dried, crumbled
- ¼ teaspoon salt
- Cooking spray
- 1 1-pound boneless top sirloin steak, about 1 inch thick, all visible fat discarded
- 1 teaspoon bottled minced garlic or 2 medium garlic cloves, minced

Directions:

- In a small bowl, stir together the tomatoes, carrots, green onion, basil, and salt. Put aside.
- Preheat the broiler. Lightly spray the broiler pan and rack with cooking oil spray.
- Cut the beef in half crosswise. Cut a large slit widthwise in each half (*almost*all the way through) to form a deep pocket. Spoon the tomato mixture into the pockets. Secure the openings with wooden toothpicks. Sprinkle the garlic over the top of the beef.
- Broil about 4 inches from the heat for 6 minutes. Turn over. Broil for 6 to 8 minutes or to the desired doneness. Transfer the beef to a cutting board. Discard the toothpicks. Cut each piece of beef in half.

7.9 Sirloin with Orange-Coriander Glaze

Servings: 4 persons

Preparation time: 5 minutes

Cooking Time: 15 minutes

Nutritional information: (Per Serving): Calories 148, Total Fat 4.5 g, Carbohydrates 2 g, Protein 24 g

Ingredients:

- ¼ cup frozen orange juice concentrate
- ½ teaspoon ground coriander
- ½ teaspoon garlic powder
- 1/8 teaspoon pepper
- 1/8 teaspoon cayenne

- 1 1-pound boneless top sirloin steak, all visible fat discarded, cut into 4 pieces
- Cooking spray
- 1/8 teaspoon salt

Directions:

- In a small bowl, stir together the orange juice concentrate, coriander, garlic powder, pepper, and cayenne. Pour about half the mixture into a separate small bowl.
- Put the beef in a shallow glass dish. Brush the top side of the beef with all the orange juice mixture from one bowl. Cover the beef and refrigerate for 10 minutes. Put aside the remaining orange juice mixture.
- About 20 minutes before serving time, preheat the broiler. Lightly spray the broiler pan and rack with cooking oil spray.
- Transfer the beef to the rack.
- Broil the beef with the seasoned side up about 4 inches from the heat for 8 minutes. Turnover. Using a clean basting brush, brush the top side with the remaining orange juice mixture. Broil for 8 to 10 minutes or to the desired doneness.
- Transfer the beef to a cutting board. Thinly slice on the diagonal. Sprinkle with salt.

7.10 Beef Fajitas in Lettuce Wraps

Servings: 4 persons

Preparation time: 10 to 12 minutes

Cooking Time: 10 to 12 minutes

Nutritional information: (Per Serving): Calories 185, Total Fat 3.5 g, Carbohydrates 14 g, Protein 23 g

Ingredients:

- Cooking spray
- ounces boneless top round steak, all visible fat discarded, thinly cut against the grain into strips 2 to 3 inches long
- 1 teaspoon canola or corn oil
- 1 large onion, thinly sliced
- 1 medium red, yellow, or green bell pepper, cut into strips
- 1 teaspoon bottled minced garlic or 2 medium garlic cloves, minced
- 2 tablespoons fresh lime juice
- 1/2 teaspoon ground cumin
- 1/4 teaspoon salt
- medium romaine or leaf lettuce leaves
- 1/2 cup fat-free sour cream

Directions:

- Lightly spray a large skillet with cooking oil spray. Heat over medium-high heat. Cook the beef for 2 to 3 minutes or to the desired doneness, stirring frequently. Transfer to a plate. Wipe the skillet with paper towels if needed.
- Pour the oil into the skillet, swirling to coat the bottom. Brown the onions, bell pepper, and garlic, still over medium-high heat, for 3 minutes, or till the onion is soft, stirring frequently. Return the beef to the skillet.
- Stir in the lime juice, cumin, and salt. Cook for 3 minutes, or until heated through.
- Spoon the beef mixture onto the center of each lettuce leaf. Top with sour cream. Fold the lettuce around the filling.

7.11 Moroccan Beef and Barley

Servings: 4 persons

Preparation time: 10 minutes

Cooking Time: 1 hour 40 minutes

Nutritional information: (Per Serving): Calories 303, Total Fat 3.0 g, Carbohydrates 44 g, Protein 26 g

Ingredients:

- Cooking spray

- ounces boneless round steak, all visible fat discarded, cut into bite-size pieces
- 2 14.5-ounce cans of no-salt-added diced tomatoes, undrained
- 1½ cups water
- 1 small onion, sliced and separated into rings
- ½ cup uncooked medium pearl barley
- 1 teaspoon sugar
- 1 teaspoon ground cumin
- 1 teaspoon ground ginger
- 1 teaspoon bottled minced garlic or 2 medium garlic cloves, minced
- ½ teaspoon ground turmeric
- ½ teaspoon paprika
- ½ teaspoon ground cinnamon
- ¼ teaspoon salt
- 10 ounces frozen mixed **vegetables, any combination**

Directions:

- Lightly spray the Dutch oven with cooking oil spray. Heat over medium-high heat. Cook the beef for 5 minutes, or until browned, stirring frequently.
- Stir in the remaining ingredients except for the mixed vegetables. Increase the heat to high and bring it to a boil. Reduce the heat and simmer, covered, for 1 hour.
- Stir in the mixed vegetables. Return to a simmer and simmer, covered, for 30 minutes, or till the beef, barley, and vegetables are tender and the liquid is absorbed. Stir before serving.

7.12 Easy Oven Beef Stew

Servings: 6 persons

Preparation time: 13 minutes

Cooking Time: 2 hours

Nutritional information: (Per Serving): Calories 266, Total Fat 3.0 g, Carbohydrates 28 g, Protein 30 g

Ingredients:

- Cooking spray
- ¼ cup all-purpose flour
- ¼ teaspoon salt
- ¼ teaspoon pepper
- 1½ pounds boneless round steak, all visible fat discarded, cut into ½-inch cubes
- cups water
- 2 medium potatoes, cut into bite-size pieces
- ounces frozen whole baby carrots
- ounces pre-sliced button mushrooms (about 2½ cups)
- 1 cup frozen pearl onions
- 1 tablespoon plus 1 teaspoon very low sodium beef bouillon granules
- 1 teaspoon dried savory or thyme, crumbled
- ½ teaspoon garlic powder

Directions:

- Heat the oven to 350°F. Lightly spray the Dutch oven with cooking oil spray.
- In a large bowl, stir together the flour, salt, and pepper. Add the beef, turning to coat. Shake off any excess. Transfer to the Dutch oven.
- Stir in the remaining ingredients.
- Bake, covered, for 2 hours, or till the beef is tender, stirring once or twice.

7.13 Quick-Fix Chicken-Fried Steak

Servings: 4 persons

Preparation time: 10 minutes

Cooking Time: 15 minutes

Nutritional information: (Per Serving): Calories 236, Total Fat 5.0 g, Carbohydrates 16 g, Protein 30 g

Ingredients:

- ½ cup low-fat buttermilk
- ½ cup all-purpose flour
- 1 teaspoon smoked paprika

- ½ teaspoon garlic powder
- ½ teaspoon salt
- ½ teaspoon pepper
- cube steaks (about 4 ounces each), all visible fat discarded
- 2 teaspoons olive oil
- ¾ cup fat-free milk

Directions:

- Pour the buttermilk into a medium-sized shallow dish.
- Flour, paprika, garlic powder, salt, as well as pepper should be mixed in a pie pan. Take 1 teaspoonful of the mixture and set it aside.
- When you're ready to cook, line up the dish, pie pan, and big plate. One piece of meat should be doused in buttermilk and dipped, turning to coat. Gently shake off any extra flour after dipping in the flour mixture. Put it on a serving dish. Continue with the rest of the meat.
- Make sure to stir the oil around to ensure it covers the bottom of the pan before putting it on medium-high heat and cooking for several minutes. 4 to 5 mins on each side, or until the exterior is browned and the center is done. Place on a big dish and serve immediately. To stay warm, cover-up.
- In a separate dish, whisk together the milk and 1 tablespoon of the flour mixture. Scrape the browned pieces from the bottom of the pan with a spatula as you pour. Over medium-high heat, stir the mixture continually until it reaches a boil. Reduce the temperature to a simmer. Whisk the gravy periodically while it cooks for 1 to 2 minutes or until it thickens. The steak is ready to be smothered with sauce.

7.14 Espresso Minute Steaks

Servings: 4 persons

Preparation time: 5 minutes

Cooking Time: 8 minutes

Nutritional information: (Per Serving): Calories 158, Total Fat 5.0 g, Carbohydrates 1 g, Protein 26 g

Ingredients:

- ½ cup strong coffee, or 1 teaspoon instant coffee granules dissolved in ½ cup water
- 2 teaspoons Worcestershire sauce (lowest sodium available)
- 2 teaspoons balsamic vinegar
- ¼ teaspoon salt
- 1 teaspoon canola or corn oil and 1 teaspoon canola or corn oil, divided use
- minute steaks or thin round steaks (about 4 ounces each), all visible fat discarded
- 2 tablespoons finely chopped green onions (optional)

Directions:

- In a small bowl, stir together the coffee, Worcestershire sauce, vinegar, and salt. Put aside.
- In a large nonstick pan, heat 1 teaspoon oil over medium-high heat, swirling to coat the bottom. Cook 2 steaks for 1 minute. Turnover. Cook for 30 seconds, or until barely pink in the center. Transfer to a platter. Cover to keep warm. Repeat with the remaining 1 teaspoon oil and remaining steaks.
- Stir the coffee mixture into the pan drippings, scraping to dislodge any browned bits. Bring to a boil over medium-high heat. Boil for 3 minutes, or till the mixture is reduced to 2 tablespoons, stirring frequently. Pour over the beef. Sprinkle with green onions.

7.15 Cajun Meat Loaf

Servings: 4 persons

Preparation time: 10 minutes

Cooking Time: 45 minutes

Nutritional information: (Per Serving): Calories 152, Total Fat 4.5 g, Carbohydrates 9 g, Protein 19 g

Ingredients:

- Cooking spray
- 1 pound extra-lean ground beef
- ½ cup chopped onion
- 1 medium rib of celery, chopped
- ½ medium red, yellow, or green bell pepper, chopped
- ½ cup plain dry breadcrumbs (lowest sodium available)
- 2 large egg whites
- 1 tablespoon Worcestershire sauce (lowest sodium available)
- 1 teaspoon salt-free Cajun seasoning blend
- ½ teaspoon ground cumin
- ¼ teaspoon salt
- ¼ teaspoon pepper
- ¼ teaspoon cayenne

Directions:

- Heat the oven to 350°F. Lightly spray a 9-inch square baking pan with cooking oil spray.
- In a large bowl, using your hands or a spoon, combine all the ingredients. Shape into a loaf about 8 × 5 inches. Transfer to the baking pan.
- Bake for 45 minutes, or till the meatloaf registers 165°F on an instant-read thermometer and is no longer pink in the center. Remove from the oven. Let stand for 5 minutes before slicing.

7.16 Healthy Joes with Pasta

Servings: 4 persons

Preparation time: 10 minutes

Cooking Time: 15 minutes

Nutritional information: (Per Serving): Calories 401, Total Fat 7.0 g, Carbohydrates 59 g, Protein 29 g

Ingredients:

- ounces uncooked whole-grain spaghetti
- ounces extra-lean ground beef
- 1 cup chopped onion
- 1 medium red, yellow, or green bell pepper, chopped
- 1½ cups meatless spaghetti sauce (lowest sodium available)
- 1 medium zucchini, shredded
- 1 tablespoon chili powder
- 1 teaspoon paprika
- ½ teaspoon bottled minced garlic or 1 medium garlic clove, minced
- 1/8 teaspoon salt

Directions:

- Prepare the pasta using the package directions, omitting the salt. Drain well in a colander. Transfer to a serving bowl and cover to keep warm. Put aside.
- Meanwhile, in a large skillet, cook the beef, onion, and bell pepper over high heat for 7 minutes, or till the beef is browned on the outside and no longer pink in the center, occasionally stirring to turn and break up the beef.
- Stir in the remaining ingredients. Bring to a boil over high heat. Reduce the heat and simmer for 5 minutes. Spoon over the pasta.

7.17 Southwest Shepherd's Pie

Servings: 8 persons

Preparation time: 8 to 10 minutes

Cooking Time: 40 to 45 minutes

Nutritional information: (Per Serving): Calories 218, Total Fat 2.5 g, Carbohydrates 36 g, Protein 15 g

Ingredients:

- ounces extra-lean ground beef
- ½ cup chopped onion
- 2 cups uncooked packaged instant mashed potatoes
- 2 cups water and ¼ cup water, divided use
- ¾ cup fat-free milk
- 1 15.5-ounce can no-salt-added kidney beans, rinsed and drained
- 1 12-ounce can no-salt-add whole-kernel corn, drained
- 1 10¾-ounce can low-fat condensed tomato soup (lowest sodium available)
- 1 4-ounce can chop green chiles, drained
- 1 teaspoon ground cumin
- 1/8 teaspoon salt
- 1/8 teaspoon pepper
- ¼ cup shredded fat-free Cheddar cheese

Directions:

- Heat the oven to 375°F.
- In a large skillet, cook the beef and onion over high heat for 5 mins, or till the beef is browned on the outside and the onion is soft, occasionally stirring to turn and break up the beef.
- Meanwhile, prepare the potatoes using the package directions, using 2 cups water and ¾ cup milk and omitting any margarine and salt.
- Stir the beans, corn, soup, chiles, cumin, salt, pepper, and remaining ¼ cup water into the beef mixture. Cook for 7 minutes, or until heated through, stirring occasionally. Transfer to a 2-quart casserole dish.
- Drop the potato mixture in mounds or spread it over the beef mixture.
- Bake for 25 to 30 minutes, or until hot. Sprinkle with the Cheddar.

7.18 Pork Roast with Horseradish and Herbs

Servings: 4 persons

Preparation time: 5 minutes

Cooking Time: 1 hour

Nutritional information: (Per Serving): Calories 135, Total Fat 5.5 g, Carbohydrates 0 g, Protein 19 g

Ingredients:

- 1 2-pound boneless pork rib roast or loin roast, all visible fat discarded
- 1 teaspoon bottled white horseradish, drained
- ½ teaspoon dried marjoram, crumbled
- ½ teaspoon dried basil, crumbled
- ½ teaspoon of dried oregano, crumbled
- ¼ teaspoon salt

Directions:

- Heat the oven to 350°F.
- Put the pork in a shallow baking pan. Spread the horseradish over the top of the pork.
- In a small bowl, stir together the marjoram, basil, oregano, and salt. Sprinkle over the horseradish.
- Roast for 1 hour, or till the pork registers 145°F on an instant-read thermometer.
- Remove from the oven and let stand for 3 minutes, or till the desired doneness is.

7.19 Pork and Rhubarb Bake

Servings: 4 persons

Preparation time: 10 minutes

Cooking Time: 30 minutes

Nutritional information: (Per Serving): Calories 207, Total Fat 5.5 g, Carbohydrates 20 g, Protein 20 g

Ingredients:

- Cooking spray
- ounces boneless pork loin roast or chops, all visible fat discarded, cut into bite-size pieces
- 1 to 1½ pounds rhubarb, cut into bite-size pieces (about 3 cups), or 16 ounces frozen unsweetened cut rhubarb, thawed and drained if frozen
- ¼ cup sugar
- 2 tablespoons all-purpose flour
- ½ teaspoon ground cinnamon
- ¼ teaspoon salt

Directions:

- Heat the oven to 350°F. Lightly spray a large skillet with cooking oil spray.
- Heat the skillet over medium-high heat. Cook the pork for 5 minutes, or until browned, stirring frequently.
- In a large bowl, stir together the remaining ingredients. Spoon half the rhubarb mixture into a 1½-quart casserole dish. Spoon the pork over the rhubarb mixture. Top with the remaining rhubarb mixture.
- Bake, covered, for 20 to 25 minutes, or till the pork is the desired doneness, and the rhubarb is tender.

7.20 Hearty Pork and Onion Stew

Servings: 4 persons

Preparation time: 15 minutes

Cooking Time: 1 hour and 15 minutes

Nutritional information: (Per Serving): Calories 285, Total Fat 7.5 g, Carbohydrates 22 g, Protein 29 g

Ingredients:

- 1/3 cup all-purpose flour
- ¼ teaspoon salt
- 1/8 teaspoon pepper
- 1½ pounds boneless pork loin roast, all visible fat discarded, cut into ½-inch cubes
- 16 ounces frozen pearl onions
- 1 12-ounce can light beer or nonalcoholic beer
- 1¼ cups fat-free, low-sodium chicken broth
- 10 ounces frozen chopped spinach, slightly thawed, broken into chunks
- 2 tablespoons red wine vinegar
- 1 tablespoon firmly packed brown sugar
- 1 teaspoon caraway seeds
- 1 teaspoon bottled minced garlic or 2 medium garlic cloves, minced
- 1 medium-dried bay leaf

Directions:

- Heat the oven to 350°F. Lightly spray a Dutch oven or a 3-quart glass casserole dish with cooking oil spray.
- In a large bowl, stir together the flour, salt, and pepper. Add half the pork, turning to coat and gently shaking off any excess. Transfer the pork to the Dutch oven. Repeat with the remaining pork.
- Stir in the remaining ingredients.
- Bake, covered, for 1 hour 30 minutes, or till the pork is tender and the desired doneness, stirring occasionally. Discard the bay leaf before serving the stew.

7.21 Three-Pepper Pork

Servings: 4 persons

Preparation time: 12 minutes

Cooking Time: 12 minutes

Nutritional information: (Per Serving): Calories 219, Total Fat 8.5 g, Carbohydrates 9 g, Protein 26 g

Ingredients:

- Cooking spray
- 1-pound boneless pork loin roast or chops, all visible fat discarded, cut into strips
- 1 medium red bell pepper, cut into strips
- 1 medium yellow bell pepper, cut into strips
- 1 medium poblano pepper, chopped
- 1 tablespoon sugar
- 1 tablespoon soy sauce (lowest sodium available)
- 1 teaspoon peeled grated gingerroot
- 1 teaspoon toasted sesame oil
- 1 teaspoon plain rice wine vinegar

Directions:

- Lightly spray a large skillet with cooking oil spray. Heat over medium-high heat. Cook the pork for 5 minutes, or until slightly pink in the center, stirring occasionally.
- Stir in all the peppers. Cook for 3 minutes, or till the peppers are tender-crisp, stirring occasionally.
- In a small bowl, stir together the remaining ingredients. Stir into the pork mixture. Cook for 2 minutes, or until heated through, stirring constantly.

7.22 Sesame Pork Tenderloin

Servings: 4 persons

Preparation time: 7 minutes

Cooking Time: 40 to 45 minutes

Nutritional information: (Per Serving): Calories 147, Total Fat 3.5 g, Carbohydrates 3 g, Protein 24 g

Ingredients:

- Cooking spray
- 1½ pounds pork tenderloin, all visible fat discarded
- 1 tablespoon light molasses
- 1 tablespoon soy sauce (lowest sodium available)
- ¼ teaspoon toasted sesame oil
- 1 tablespoon sesame seeds

Directions:

- Heat the oven to 425°F. Lightly spray a large shallow baking pan with cooking oil spray.
- Put the pork in the baking pan.
- In a small bowl, stir together the molasses, soy sauce, and sesame oil. Brush all over the pork. Sprinkle the pork with the sesame seeds.
- Roast for 40 to 45 minutes, or till the pork registers 145°F on an instant-read thermometer.
- Remove from the oven and let stand for 3 minutes, or till the desired doneness is.
- Cut crosswise into slices.

7.23 Pesto Pork Pinwheels

Servings: 4 persons

Preparation time: 8 to 10 minutes

Cooking Time: 30 to 35 minutes

Nutritional information: (Per Serving): Calories 136, Total Fat 3.5 g, Carbohydrates 0 g, Protein 24 g

Ingredients:

- 1 1-pound pork tenderloin, all visible fat discarded, butterflied, and flattened to the ¼-inch thickness
- 1 tablespoon Crunchy Basil-Parmesan Pesto or commercial pesto (lowest sodium available)

Directions:

- Heat the oven to 425°F.
- Lay the pork flat. Spread the pesto over the pork. Roll up from one of the short ends and tie with string in several places to secure. Transfer to a medium shallow baking pan.
- Roast for 30 to 35 minutes, or till the pork registers 145°F on an instant-read thermometer. Remove from the oven and let stand for 3 minutes, or till the desired doneness is. Cut crosswise into slices.

7.24 Pork Medallions with Sautéed Mushrooms

Servings: 4 persons

Preparation time: 10 minutes

Cooking Time: 15 minutes

Nutritional information: (Per Serving): Calories 151, Total Fat 4.0 g, Carbohydrates 3 g, Protein 26 g

Ingredients:

- Cooking spray
- 1 1-pound pork tenderloin, all visible fat discarded, cut into 12 slices and flattened to the ¾-inch thickness
- 3-4 ounces pre-sliced button mushrooms (about 2½ cups)
- 2 medium green onions, sliced
- 1 tablespoon light tub margarine
- 1 teaspoon finely snipped fresh rosemary or ¼ teaspoon dried, crushed
- ¼ teaspoon salt
- 1 tablespoon dry sherry (optional)

Directions:

- Spray a big skillet with cooking spray. Preheat over a medium-high heat source. Cook half the pork for 3 minutes on each side, or until it registers 145°F on an instant-read thermometer. Transfer to a large plate. Cover to keep warm. Repeat with the remaining pork.
- In the same skillet, cook the remaining ingredients except for the sherry over medium heat for 2 to 3 minutes, or till the mushrooms are soft, stirring occasionally. Stir in the sherry. Spoon over the pork.

7.25 Maple-Bourbon Pork Medallions

Servings: 4 persons

Preparation time: 7 minutes

Cooking Time: 18 minutes

Nutritional information: (Per Serving): Calories 256, Total Fat 3.0 g, Carbohydrates 21 g, Protein 24 g

Ingredients:

- 1/3 cup maple syrup
- 1/3 cup bourbon or unsweetened apple juice
- 2 tablespoons whole-grain or Dijon mustard (lowest sodium available)
- 2 tablespoons no-salt-added ketchup
- Cooking spray
- 1 1-pound pork tenderloin, all visible fat discarded, cut into 12 slices and flattened to the ¾-inch thickness

Directions:

- In a small bowl, stir together the maple syrup, bourbon, mustard, and ketchup. Put aside.
- Spray a medium-sized pan with cooking spray and heat it at a medium-high level. Cook half the pork for 3 minutes on each side, or until it registers 145°F on an instant-read thermometer. Transfer to a plate. Cover to keep warm. Repeat with the remaining pork.
- In the same skillet, cook the syrup mixture, still over medium-high heat, for 4 minutes, or until bubbly, stirring frequently.
- Cook for 1 to 2 minutes, or until thickened

to the desired consistency, stirring constantly. Spoon over the pork.

7.26 Pork Chops with Honey-Lemon Sauce

Servings: 4 persons

Preparation time: 5 minutes

Cooking Time: 20 minutes

Nutritional information: (Per Serving): Calories 255, Total Fat 8.0 g, Carbohydrates 19 g, Protein 26 g

Ingredients:

- boneless pork loin chops (about 4 ounces each), ½ to ¾ inch thick, all visible fat discarded, halved
- ¼ cup honey
- ¼ cup fresh lemon juice
- 2 tablespoons soy sauce (lowest sodium available)
- ½ teaspoon bottled minced garlic or 1 medium garlic clove, minced

Directions:

- Spray a medium-sized pan with cooking spray and heat it. Medium-high heat is ideal. Cook the pork for 1 minute on each side. Reduce the heat to medium. Cook for 8 minutes. Turnover. Cook for 5 minutes, or till the pork registers 145°F on an instant-read thermometer. Transfer to a large plate. Cover to keep warm.
- Meanwhile, in a small bowl, stir together the sauce ingredients. Put aside.
- When the pork is done, pour the sauce into the same skillet. Cook over high heat for 3 minutes or until thickened to the desired consistency, stirring occasionally. Spoon over the pork

7.27 Tropical Pork Chops

Servings: 4 persons

Preparation time: 10 minutes

Cooking Time: 10 minutes

Nutritional information: (Per Serving): Calories 156, Total Fat 7.0 g, Carbohydrates 0 g, Protein 21 g

Ingredients:

- ½ cup fat-free, low-sodium chicken broth
- ½ cup pineapple juice
- 2 tablespoons firmly packed light brown sugar
- 2 tablespoons fresh lime juice
- ½ teaspoon ground ginger
- ¼ teaspoon ground cloves
- ¼ teaspoon salt
- ¼ teaspoon bottled minced garlic or ½ medium garlic clove, minced
- 1/8 teaspoon ground nutmeg
- 1/8 teaspoon crushed red pepper flakes
- boneless pork loin chops (about 4 ounces each), about ¾ inch thick, all visible fat discarded
- Cooking spray

Directions:

- In a large shallow glass dish, stir together the marinade ingredients. Add the pork, turning to coat. Cover and refrigerate for about 24 hours, turning occasionally.
- About 20 minutes before serving time, lightly spray the broiler pan and rack with cooking oil spray. Preheat the broiler.
- Drain the pork, discarding the marinade.
- Broil the pork about 4 inches from the heat for 4 minutes. Turnover and broil for 3 to 5 minutes, or until it registers 145°F on an instant-read thermometer. Remove from the broiler. Let stand for 3 minutes, or till the desired doneness.

7.28 Pork Chop and Sweet Potato Skillet

Servings: 4 persons

Preparation time: 10 minutes

Cooking Time: 40 minutes

Nutritional information: (Per Serving): Calories 260, Total Fat 6.5 g, Carbohydrates 23 g, Protein 26 g

Ingredients:

- 4 ounces of boneless pork loin chops, half to ¾ inch thick
- 1 large, sweet potato, chopped
- 1 medium onion, chopped
- 1 15.5-ounces of no-salt-add stewed tomatoes, undrained
- Half teaspoon dried basil, crumbled
- Half teaspoon dried oregano, crumbled
- Half teaspoon bottled minced garlic or 1 medium garlic clove, minced
- Quarter teaspoon salt

Directions:

Spray a medium-sized pan with cooking spray and heat it. Medium-high heat is ideal. Cook the pork for 5 minutes on each side or until browned. Remove from the skillet.

Put the sweet potato and onion in the skillet. Place the pork on top. Pour in the tomatoes with liquid. Sprinkle with basil, oregano, garlic, and salt. Increase the heat to high and bring it to a boil. Reduce the heat and simmer, covered, for 25 minutes, or till the sweet potato is tender and the pork registers 145°F on an instant-read thermometer. Remove from the heat. Let stand, uncovered, for 3 minutes.

7.29 Double-Apricot and Ham Kebabs

Servings: 4 persons

Preparation time: 15 minutes

Cooking Time: 15 minutes

Nutritional information: (Per Serving): Calories 195, Total Fat 2.0 g, Carbohydrates 34 g, Protein 10 g

Ingredients:

- ¼ cup all-fruit apricot spread
- 1 tablespoon white wine vinegar or cider vinegar
- ¼ teaspoon dry mustard
- ounces lower-sodium, low-fat ham, all visible fat discarded, cut into 16 bite-size cubes
- 16 pineapple chunks from one 20-ounce can pineapple chunks in their juice, drained
- 16 dried apricot halves
- 1 medium red bell pepper, cut into 16 squares

Directions:

- Soak eight 10-inch wooden skewers in cold water for at least 10 minutes to keep them from charring or use metal skewers.
- Heat the oven to 450°F.
- In a small saucepan, stir together the apricot spread, vinegar, and mustard. Cook over low heat while preparing the kebabs, stirring occasionally.
- On each skewer, thread 1 ham chunk, 1 pineapple chunk, 1 apricot half, and 1 bell pepper piece. Repeat. Transfer to a shallow glass baking dish large enough to hold the kebabs in a single layer. Brush the kebabs with the apricot mixture, reserving any remaining.
- Bake the kebabs for 15 minutes, occasionally brushing with any remaining apricot mixture.

7.30 Rosemary Lamb Chops with Lemon Sauce

Servings: 4 persons

Preparation time: 10 to 12 minutes

Cooking Time: 10 minutes

Nutritional information: (Per Serving): Calories 152, Total Fat 6.5 g, Carbohydrates 1 g, Protein 20 g

Ingredients:

- Cooking spray
- 1 tablespoon finely snipped fresh rosemary or 1 teaspoon dried, crushed
- boneless lamb leg sirloin chops (about 4 ounces each), about ¾ inch thick, all visible fat discarded
- 1/3 cup fat-free, low-sodium chicken broth
- 1 teaspoon cornstarch
- ¼ teaspoon grated lemon zest
- 1 tablespoon fresh lemon juice
- 1 teaspoon Dijon mustard (lowest sodium available)
- ¼ teaspoon salt

Directions:

- Preheat the broiler. Lightly spray the broiler pan and rack with cooking oil spray.
- Sprinkle the rosemary over both sides of the lamb. Using your fingertips, gently press the rosemary, so it adheres to the lamb.
- Broil the lamb about 4 inches from the heat for 5 to 6 minutes. Turn over. Broil for 3 to 5 minutes or to the desired doneness.
- Meanwhile, in a small saucepan, whisk together the broth and cornstarch. Whisk in the lemon zest, lemon juice, mustard, and salt. Cook over medium heat for 5 mins or until thickened to the desired consistency, whisking constantly. Serve over the lamb.

7.31 Curried Lamb Stroganoff

Servings: 4 persons

Preparation time: 10 minutes

Cooking Time: 18 minutes

Nutritional information: (Per Serving): Calories 289, Total Fat 5.5 g, Carbohydrates 38 g, Protein 22 g

Ingredients:

- 1 cup uncooked instant brown rice
- ¼ cup raisins or dried currants
- ounces lean ground lamb
- 1 medium Granny Smith or another tart apple, peeled and chopped
- 1 small onion, chopped
- ¾ cup fat-free, low-sodium chicken broth
- 1 tablespoon plus 1 to 2 teaspoons curry powder
- 1 teaspoon bottled minced garlic or 2 medium garlic cloves, minced
- ¼ teaspoon salt
- ¼ teaspoon ground cinnamon
- 1/8 teaspoon pepper
- ¼ cup fat-free sour cream or fat-free plain yogurt
- 1 tablespoon all-purpose flour

Directions:

- Prepare the rice using the package directions, omitting the salt and margarine and adding the raisins.
- Meanwhile, in a large skillet, cook the lamb over high heat for 7 minutes, or until brown, occasionally stirring to turn and break up the lamb. Drain well. Return to the skillet.
- Stir the apple, onion, broth, curry powder, garlic, salt, cinnamon, and pepper into the lamb. Increase the heat to high and bring it to a boil. Reduce the heat and simmer, covered, for 5 minutes.
- In a small bowl, whisk the sour cream and flour. Stir into the lamb mixture. Cook over low heat for 3 minutes, or till the desired consistency, stirring constantly. Serve over the rice mixture.

7.32 Kiwi Veal

Servings: 4 persons

Preparation time: 5 minutes

Cooking Time: 5 minutes

Nutritional information: (Per Serving): Calories 232, Total Fat 2.0 g, Carbohydrates 29 g, Protein 24 g

Ingredients:

- ½ cup tomato preserves
- 1 medium kiwifruit, peeled and chopped
- ¼ teaspoon salt
- Cooking spray
- 1 pound veal scaloppine, cut about ¼ inch thick

Directions:

- In a small saucepan, stir together the tomato preserves, kiwifruit, and salt. Cook over low heat for 3 minutes or until heated through, stirring occasionally.
- Meanwhile, Spray a medium-sized pan with cooking spray and heat it. Medium-high heat is ideal so keep heating. Cook the veal for 2 minutes on each side or until tender. Serve topped with the sauce.

7.33 Veal Scaloppine in Shiitake Cream Sauce

Servings: 4 persons

Preparation time: 10 minutes

Cooking Time: 19 minutes

Nutritional information: (Per Serving): Calories 226, Total Fat 2.5 g, Carbohydrates 17 g, Protein 33 g

Ingredients:

- 1 pound veal scaloppine, cut about ¼ inch thick
- ounces shiitake mushroom stems discarded, sliced, or pre-sliced button mushrooms
- medium green onions, sliced
- 1 teaspoon bottled minced garlic or 2 medium garlic cloves, minced
- 2 teaspoons all-purpose flour
- ½ teaspoon chopped fresh thyme or ¼ teaspoon dried, crumbled
- ¼ teaspoon salt
- 1/8 teaspoon pepper
- 1 12-ounce can fat-free evaporated milk
- 1 tablespoon dry sherry (optional)

Directions:

- Spray a medium-sized pan with cooking spray and heat it. Medium-high heat is ideal. Cook the veal for 2 minutes on each side or until tender. Transfer to a large plate. Cover to keep warm.
- Lightly spray the same skillet with cooking oil spray. Cook the mushrooms, green onions, and garlic over medium heat for 5 mins, or till the mushrooms are soft, stirring occasionally.
- Stir in the flour, thyme, salt, and pepper. Pour in the evaporated milk all at once, stirring to combine. Cook for 4 minutes, or till the desired consistency, stirring constantly. Stir in the sherry.
- Return the veal to the skillet, turning to coat. Cook for 3 minutes, or until heated through.

Chapter 8 Vegetarian Entrées

In addition to lowering blood pressure and decreasing the risk of cardiovascular disease and stroke, eating a diet high in fruits and vegetables can help prevent some forms of cancer, lower the risk of eye and gastrointestinal issues, and have a positive high blood sugar level, which can help keep appetite under control. The consumption of non-starchy vegetables and fruits, such as apples and pears, as well as green leafy vegetables, may even aid in weight reduction. Their low glycemic indexes help to reduce blood sugar surges, which may lead to an increase in appetite.

8.1 Spicy Penne with Greens and Beans

Servings: 6 persons

Preparation time: 10 minutes

Cooking Time: 25 minutes

Nutritional information: (Per Serving): Calories 326, Total Fat 2.5 g, Carbohydrates 62 g, Protein 15 g

Ingredients:

- 3 quarts water and ½ cup water, divided to use
- ounces collard greens, any large stems discarded, chopped (about 5 cups)
- ounces dried whole-grain penne (about 3 cups)
- 2 teaspoons olive oil
- ½ cup chopped onion
- 1 medium carrot, sliced
- 1 teaspoon finely snipped fresh rosemary
- 1 teaspoon snipped fresh thyme
- ½ teaspoon crushed red pepper flakes
- 2 15.5-ounce cans of no-salt-added black beans, rinsed and drained
- 2 cups no-salt-added crushed tomatoes, undrained
- ¼ cup balsamic vinegar
- ½ teaspoon salt
- Red hot-pepper sauce to taste (optional

Directions:

- In a soup pot, bring 3 quarts of water and the collard greens to a boil, covered, over high heat. Stir in the pasta. Cook, uncovered, using the package directions and omitting the salt. Drain well in a colander.
- Meanwhile, in a large skillet, heat the oil over medium-high heat, swirling to coat the bottom. Brown the onions, carrot, rosemary, thyme, and red pepper flakes for 3 to 4 minutes, or till the onion is soft, stirring frequently.
- Stir in the bean tomatoes with liquid, vinegar, salt, and remaining ½ cup water. Reduce the heat to medium-low. Cook for 3 minutes, or until heated through, stirring frequently. Remove from the heat.
- Stir in the pasta mixture. Serve with the hot-pepper sauce.

8.2 Rotini with Creamy Basil-Edamame Sauce

Servings: 4 persons

Preparation time: 12 minutes

Cooking Time: 11 minutes

Nutritional information: (Per Serving): Calories 316, Total Fat 6.5 g, Carbohydrates 51 g, Protein 17 g

Ingredients:

- ounces dried whole-grain rotini or Rotella pasta (about 3 cups)
- 6 ounces frozen shelled edamame (green soybeans), thawed
- ½ cup loosely packed fresh basil (about ¾ ounce)

- ¼ cup low-fat ricotta cheese
- 1 tablespoon fresh lemon juice
- 1 teaspoon bottled minced garlic or 2 medium garlic cloves, minced
- 1 teaspoon olive oil and 1 teaspoon olive oil, divided use
- ¼ teaspoon salt
- 1 tablespoon water (if needed)
- ounces sliced baby belle mushrooms (about 2½ cups)
- 1 cup chopped onion
- 2 tablespoons crumbled fat-free feta cheese

Directions:

- Prepare the pasta using the package directions, omitting the salt. Drain well in a colander.
- Meanwhile, in a food processor or blender, process the edamame, basil, ricotta, lemon juice, garlic, 1 teaspoon oil, and the salt for 40 seconds, or until smooth, scraping the side of the bowl once. If the mixture is too thick, add the water and process until blended. Put aside.
- In a nonstick pan, heat the remaining 1 teaspoon oil over medium-high heat, swirling to coat the bottom. Cook the mushrooms and onion for 3 minutes, or until soft, stirring frequently. Transfer to a large bowl.
- Add the pasta and the edamame mixture to the mushroom mixture, stirring gently to coat. Serve sprinkled with feta.

8.3 Tangy Yogurt-Tomato Fusilli

Servings: 4 persons

Preparation time: 8 minutes

Cooking Time: 13 to 15 minutes

Nutritional information: (Per Serving): Calories 302, Total Fat 3.5 g, Carbohydrates 52 g, Protein 17 g

Ingredients:

- 8 ounces dried whole-grain fusilli (about 3½ cups)
- 1 14.5-ounce can no-salt-add diced tomatoes, undrained
- 1 teaspoon bottled minced garlic or 2 medium garlic cloves, minced
- 1 teaspoon dried rosemary, crushed
- 1 cup frozen shelled edamame (green soybeans)
- 2 teaspoons capers, drained and chopped
- ½ teaspoon grated lemon zest
- ¼ teaspoon salt
- ¼ teaspoon pepper

Directions:

- Prepare the pasta using the package directions, omitting the salt. Drain well in a colander. Transfer to a large bowl.
- Meanwhile, in a large nonstick skillet, cook the tomatoes with liquid, garlic, and rosemary over high heat for 5 mins, stirring occasionally.
- Stir in the remaining ingredients except for the yogurt. Bring to a simmer, still over medium-high heat. Reduce the heat and simmer for 5 to 6 minutes, or until most of the liquid has evaporated, stirring occasionally. Remove from the heat.
- Stir the yogurt into the edamame mixture. Stir into the pasta. Serve immediately to keep the pasta from absorbing the sauce.

8.4 Mediterranean Penne with Pine Nut Tomato Sauce and Feta

Servings: 4 persons

Preparation time: 11 to 13 minutes

Cooking Time: 23 to 26 minutes

Nutritional information: (Per Serving): Calories 318, Total Fat 11.5 g, Carbohydrates 43 g, Protein 14 g

Ingredients:

- 6 ounces dried whole-grain penne (about 2¼ cups)

- 1 teaspoon olive oil and 2 teaspoons olive oil, divided use
- 1 cup finely chopped onion
- 2 teaspoons bottled minced garlic or 4 medium garlic cloves, minced
- 1 14.5-ounce can no-salt-added diced tomatoes, undrained
- ¼ cup chopped fresh basil (about 2/3 ounce) or 1 tablespoon dried, crumbled
- 1 tablespoon chopped fresh oregano or 1 teaspoon dried, crumbled
- 1 teaspoon sugar
- ¼ cup pine nuts, dry-roasted
- 3 ounces crumbled low-fat feta cheese (about ¾ cup)

Directions:

- Prepare the pasta using the package directions, omitting the salt. Drain well in a colander.
- Meanwhile, in a saucepan, heat 1 teaspoon of oil over medium-high heat, swirling to coat the bottom. Brown the onions for 3 minutes, or until soft, stirring frequently.
- Stir in the garlic. Cook for 15 seconds, stirring constantly.
- Stir in the tomatoes with liquid, basil, and oregano if using dried and sugar. Bring to a simmer. Reduce the heat and simmer for 15 minutes or till the mixture is slightly thickened. Remove from the heat.
- If using fresh basil and oregano, stir them into the tomato mixture. Stir in the pine nuts and the remaining 2 teaspoons oil.
- Pour the pasta onto a platter. Sprinkle with the feta. Mound the tomato mixture on top.

8.5 Peanut Pasta and Vegetables

Servings: 4 persons

Preparation time: 10 minutes

Cooking Time: 15 minutes

Nutritional information: (Per Serving): Calories 352, Total Fat 11.5 g, Carbohydrates 52 g, Protein 14 g

Ingredients:

- ounces dried whole-grain spaghetti
- 6 ounces broccoli slaw mix (about 3 cups)
- ¼ cup creamy peanut butter (lowest sodium available)
- 3 tablespoons plain rice vinegar
- 2 tablespoons soy sauce (lowest sodium available)
- 1 tablespoon sugar
- ½ teaspoon bottled minced garlic or 1 medium garlic clove, minced
- 1/8 teaspoon cayenne
- ¼ cup chopped fresh basil (about 2/3 ounce) or snipped fresh cilantro
- 2 tablespoons chopped peanuts, dry-roasted

Directions:

- Prepare the pasta using the package directions, omitting the salt and adding the slaw mix during the last 1 minute of cooking time. Put aside 1/3 cup of the cooking liquid. Drain the pasta mixture well in a colander.
- Meanwhile, in a large bowl, whisk the peanut butter, vinegar, soy sauce, sugar, garlic, and cayenne.
- Add the hot pasta mixture to the peanut

butter mixture, stirring to coat. If the sauce is too thick, stir in the reserved cooking liquid 1 tablespoon at a time until creamy. Stir in the basil. Sprinkle with the peanuts.

8.6 Creamy Green Rice and Black Beans

Servings: 4 persons

Preparation time: 7 minutes

Cooking Time: 15 minutes

Nutritional information: (Per Serving): Calories 218, Total Fat 1.0, Carbohydrates 40 g, Protein 12 g

Ingredients:

- 1 poblano chili, quartered, seeds and ribs discarded if desired
- ½ cup coarsely chopped onion (yellow preferred)
- 1 medium garlic clove
- 3 to 4 ounces spinach (2 firmly packed cups)
- ¼ cup water (plus more as needed)
- ¼ teaspoon salt
- 1 15.5-ounce can no-salt-add black beans, rinsed and drained
- ounces frozen cooked brown rice (about 2 cups)
- ½ cup fat-free plain Greek yogurt

Directions:

- In a large nonstick skillet, cook the poblano, onion, and garlic over high heat for 8 to 10 minutes, or till the poblano is slightly blackened, stirring occasionally. Transfer to a food processor or blender.
- Add the spinach, ¼ cup water, and salt. Process until smooth, adding more water 1 tablespoon at a time as needed, processing after each addition. Return the mixture to the skillet.
- Stir in the beans. Cook over medium heat for 2 minutes or until heated through.

- Meanwhile, prepare the rice using the package directions.
- Stir the yogurt into the poblano mixture. Stir in the rice.

8.7 Three-Bean Chili

Servings: 4 persons

Preparation time: 10 to 12 minutes

Cooking Time: 21 minutes

Nutritional information: (Per Serving): Calories 276, Total Fat 3.0 g, Carbohydrates 47 g, Protein 18 g

Ingredients:

- 4 large poblano peppers
- Cooking spray
- 1 teaspoon olive oil
- 1 medium onion, chopped
- 1 tablespoon chili powder
- 1 teaspoon ground cumin
- 1 teaspoon bottled minced garlic or 2 medium garlic cloves, minced
- ¼ teaspoon salt
- 2 15.5-ounce cans of no-salt-added pinto, small red, or black beans, rinsed and drained
- 4 medium Italian plum (Roma) tomatoes, chopped
- ¼ cup snipped fresh cilantro
- ½ cup shredded low-fat Cheddar cheese
- 1 medium lime, cut into 4 wedges

Directions:

- On one side of each poblano pepper, cut a slit almost from end to end, being careful to keep the peppers intact. Transfer the peppers to a 9-inch square or round glass baking dish. Microwave, covered, on 100 percent power (high) for 10 minutes, or until tender. Remove from the microwave. Let stand, uncovered, for 10 minutes, or until cool enough to handle. Discard the ribs and seeds.
- Meanwhile, preheat the broiler. Lightly spray

- a rimmed baking sheet with cooking oil spray. Put aside.
- In a large nonstick pan, heat the oil over medium-high heat, swirling to coat the bottom. Brown the onions for 3 minutes, or until soft, stirring frequently.
- Stir in the chili powder, cumin, garlic, and salt. Cook for 1 minute, stirring frequently.
- Stir in the beans and tomatoes. Cook for 4 to 5 minutes, or till the tomatoes are softened, stirring frequently. Stir in the cilantro.
- Spoon 1 cup of the bean mixture into each pepper. Arrange the peppers in a single layer on the baking sheet. Sprinkle the peppers with Cheddar.
- Broil about 4 inches from the heat for 1 to 2 minutes, or till the Cheddar melts. Serve with the lime wedges to squeeze over the peppers.

8.8 White-Bean Veggie Burgers with Avocado Topping

Servings: 4 persons

Preparation time: 12 minutes

Cooking Time: 12 minutes

Nutritional information: (Per Serving): Calories 359, Total Fat 12.5 g, Carbohydrates 46 g, Protein 17 g

Ingredients:
- Cooking spray
- 2 15.5-ounce cans of no-salt-added navy beans, rinsed, drained, and coarsely mashed
- 1 4-ounce can chop mild green chiles
- 1/3 cup uncooked quick-cooking oatmeal
- 2 large egg whites
- 1 tablespoon plus 1 teaspoon olive oil
- 2 teaspoons smoked paprika
- 1 teaspoon bottled minced garlic or 2 medium garlic cloves, minced
- 1/8 teaspoon salt and 1/8 teaspoon salt, divided use
- 1 medium avocado, mashed
- 2 tablespoons fat-free sour cream
- 1 tablespoon fresh lime juice

Directions:
- Preheat the broiler. Line a baking sheet with aluminum foil. Lightly spray the foil with cooking oil spray.
- In a bowl, stir together the beans, chiles, oatmeal, egg whites, oil, paprika, garlic, and 1/8 teaspoon salt. Shape into 4 patties, each about 4 inches in diameter, or spoon 4 mounds of the mixture onto the baking sheet and flatten slightly to form patties. Lightly spray the tops with cooking oil spray.
- Broil the patties about 4 inches from the heat for 8 minutes. Turnover. Lightly spray the tops with cooking oil spray. Broil for 5 minutes, or until lightly browned.
- Meanwhile, in a small bowl, stir together the avocado, sour cream, lime juice, and remaining 1/8 teaspoon salt. Spoon the topping over the cooked patties.

8.9 Meatless Tamale Pie

Servings: 6 persons

Preparation time: 8 minutes

Cooking Time: 32 minutes

Nutritional information: (Per Serving): Calories 356, Total Fat 4.0 g, Carbohydrates 70 g, Protein 15 g

Ingredients:
- Cooking spray
- 1 medium carrot, chopped
- 1 cup chopped onion
- 2 15.5-ounce cans of no-salt-added kidney beans, rinsed and drained
- 1 12-ounce can no-salt-add whole-kernel corn, drained
- 1 8-ounce can no-salt-added tomato sauce
- 1 to 2 teaspoons chili powder
- 1 teaspoon ground cumin

- 1 8.5-ounce package corn muffin mix (lowest sodium available)
- 2 large egg whites
- 1/3 cup fat-free milk

Directions:

- Heat the oven to 450°F. Lightly spray a 9-inch square glass baking dish and a large skillet with cooking oil spray. Set the dish aside.
- In the skillet, cook the carrot and onion over high heat for 5 mins, or till the carrot is almost tender, stirring frequently.
- Stir in the beans, corn, tomato sauce, chili powder, and cumin. Cook for 5 minutes, or until heated through, stirring occasionally.
- Meanwhile, in a bowl, stir together the corn muffin mix, egg whites, and milk until smooth.
- Spoon the carrot mixture into the baking dish. Spread the corn muffin batter over the mixture.
- Bake for 20 minutes, or till the top is golden brown and a wooden toothpick inserted in the center comes out clean.

8.10 Double-Bean Lettuce Wraps

Servings: 4 persons

Preparation time: 8 minutes

Cooking Time: 0 minutes

Nutritional information: (Per Serving): Calories 120, Total Fat 0.0 g, Carbohydrates 22 g, Protein 8 g

Ingredients:

- 1 15.5-ounce can no-salt-add red kidney beans, rinsed, drained, and mashed
- 1 cup canned no-salt-added black beans, rinsed and drained
- 1 4-ounce can chop green chiles, drained
- 1 teaspoon ground cumin
- Bibb lettuce leaves
- ¼ cup Chunky Salsa or commercial salsa (lowest sodium available)

Directions:

- In a bowl, stir together the beans, chiles, and cumin.
- Spoon about ¼ cup bean mixture down the center of each lettuce leaf. Top with the salsa. Roll up jelly-roll style.

8.11 Vegetarian Couscous Paella

Servings: 4 persons

Preparation time: 10 to 12 minutes

Cooking Time: 15 minutes

Nutritional information: (Per Serving): Calories 315, Total Fat 1.0 g, Carbohydrates 65 g, Protein 14 g

Ingredients:

- Cooking spray
- 1 small red onion, chopped
- 2 teaspoons bottled minced garlic or 4 medium garlic cloves, minced
- 1½ cups low-sodium vegetable broth
- 9 ounces frozen baby lima beans
- 3 to 4 ounces frozen green peas
- ¼ teaspoon salt
- 1/8 teaspoon powdered saffron or ½ teaspoon ground turmeric
- 1/8 teaspoon cayenne
- 1 cup uncooked whole-wheat couscous
- 1 medium tomato, chopped
- ¼ cup snipped fresh cilantro or parsley

Directions:

- Lightly spray a large saucepan with cooking oil spray. Brown the onions and garlic over high heat for 3 minutes, or till the onion is soft, stirring frequently.
- Stir in the broth, lima beans, peas, salt, saffron, and cayenne. Increase the heat to high and bring it to a boil. Reduce the heat and simmer, covered, for 10 minutes, or till the lima beans are tender. Remove from the heat.

- Stir in the couscous, tomato, and cilantro. Let stand, covered, for 5 minutes.

8.12 Lentils with Green Beans, Carrots, and Dried Currants

Servings: 4 persons

Preparation time: 8 minutes

Cooking Time: 40 minutes

Nutritional information: (Per Serving): Calories 246, Total Fat 0.6 g, Carbohydrates 48 g, Protein 15 g

Ingredients:

- 2 cups water
- 1 cup dried green lentils, sorted for stones and shriveled lentils, rinsed, and drained
- 1 medium onion, chopped
- ¼ cup dried currants or raisins
- 1 teaspoon bottled minced garlic or 2 medium garlic cloves, minced
- ½ teaspoon curry powder
- ¼ teaspoon salt
- ¼ teaspoon pepper
- ounces frozen cut green beans
- 4 medium carrots, cut crosswise into ½-inch slices

Directions:

- In a large saucepan, bring the water, lentils, onion, currants, garlic, curry powder, salt, and pepper to a boil over high heat. Reduce the heat and simmer, covered, for 20 minutes.
- Stir in the green beans and carrots. Return to a simmer and simmer, covered, for 15 to 20 minutes, or till the lentils and vegetables are tender, stirring occasionally.

8.13 Barley and Veggie Stew with Mozzarella and Parmesan

Servings: 4 persons

Preparation time: 15 minutes

Cooking Time: 15 minutes

Nutritional information: (Per Serving): Calories 148, Total Fat 3.0 g, Carbohydrates 23 g, Protein 9 g

Ingredients:

- Cooking spray
- 2 medium red bell peppers, or 1 medium red bell pepper and 1 medium green bell pepper, cut into bite-size pieces
- 1 cup coarsely chopped onions (about 2 medium)
- 1 cup grape tomatoes, quartered
- 4 ounces green beans, trimmed and cut into 1-inch pieces
- 1½ cups water and ½ cup water, divided use
- 1/3 cup uncooked quick-cooking barley
- 1 teaspoon bottled minced garlic or 2 medium garlic cloves, minced
- ¼ cup chopped fresh basil (about 2/3 ounce)
- 1 teaspoon Louisiana hot sauce
- ¼ teaspoon salt
- ¾ cup shredded low-fat mozzarella cheese
- 1 tablespoon plus 1 teaspoon shredded or grated Parmesan cheese

Directions:

- Preheat the broiler. Line a rimmed baking sheet with aluminum foil. Lightly spray the foil with cooking oil spray.
- Arrange the bell peppers, onions, tomatoes, and green beans in a single layer on the baking sheet. Lightly spray the vegetables with cooking oil spray.
- Broil about 4 inches from the heat for 10 minutes, or till the edges are just beginning too lightly brown. Toss the vegetables, keeping them in a single layer. Broil for 5 minutes, or until richly browned on the edges.
- Meanwhile, in a saucepan, bring 1½ cups water to a boil over high heat. Stir in the barley and garlic. Return to a boil. Reduce the heat and simmer, covered, for 10 to 12 minutes, or till the barley is tender. Don't drain.

- Stir the broiled vegetables into the barley.
- Pour the remaining ½ cup water onto the foil-lined baking sheet. Gently scrape the browned bits from the foil. Pour into thebarley mixture.
- Stir in the basil, hot sauce, and salt. Serve with the mozzarella and Parmesan sprinkled on top.

8.14 Quinoa-Vegetable Patties

Servings: 4 persons

Preparation time: 10 minutes

Cooking Time: 22 to 24 minutes

Nutritional information: (Per Serving): Calories 183, Total Fat 5.5 g, Carbohydrates 27 g, Protein 9 g

Ingredients:

- ½ cup uncooked pre-rinsed quinoa
- ounces frozen chopped broccoli (about 2½ cups)
- 4 ounces frozen cut green beans (about 1½ cups)
- ½ cup low-sodium vegetable broth
- ¼ cup finely chopped onion
- 1 teaspoon bottled minced garlic or 2 medium garlic cloves, minced
- 1/3 cup toasted wheat germ
- 1 large egg
- 1 teaspoon snipped fresh dill weed, and 2 teaspoons snipped fresh dillweed, divided use
- ½ teaspoon red hot-pepper sauce
- ¼ teaspoon salt
- 2 teaspoons fresh lemon juice
- 2 teaspoons olive oil
- 1 medium tomato, cut into 4 slices
- ¼ cup fat-free plain yogurt

Directions:

- Prepare the quinoa using the package directions, omitting the salt. Spread the quinoa on a large plate to cool for 2 minutes.
- Meanwhile, in a large nonstick skillet, stir together the broccoli, green beans, broth, onion, and garlic. Cook over high heat for 7 minutes, or until most of the broth has evaporated and the vegetables are tender.
- While the broccoli mixture and quinoa cook, whisk the wheat germ, egg, 1 teaspoon of dillweed, hot-pepper sauce, and salt in a large bowl. Put aside.
- Transfer the cooked broccoli mixture to a food processor or blender. Add the lemon juice and process until smooth. Put aside. Stir the broccoli mixture and cooled quinoa into the wheat germ mixture.
- Wipe the skillet with paper towels. Heat the oil over medium-high heat, swirling to coat the bottom. Form the vegetable mixture into four 4-inch patties. Cook for 4 minutes on each side, or until well browned. Serve each patty on a tomato slice. Top with the yogurt and the remaining 2 teaspoons of dillweed.

8.15 Chickpeas and Quinoa with Mango Chutney

Servings: 4 persons

Preparation time: 10 minutes

Cooking Time: 17 minutes

Nutritional information: (Per Serving): Calories 230, Total Fat 4 g, Carbohydrates 23 g, Protein 10 g

Ingredients:

- 6 large eggs
- ¼ cup light mayonnaise
- 1 medium green onion or ¼ medium shallot, finely chopped
- 1 medium rib of celery, finely chopped
- ½ medium red bell pepper, finely chopped
- 1 tablespoon yellow mustard (lowest sodium available)
- ¼ teaspoon ground turmeric
- ¼ to ½ teaspoon paprika
- ¼ teaspoon pepper
- 2 6-inch whole-grain pita pockets, halved

- 24 baby spinach leaves

Directions:

- Put the eggs in a single layer in a large saucepan. Cover with cold water by 1 inch. Bring to a rolling boil, covered, over high heat. Remove from the heat. Let stand, covered, for 15 minutes. Drain. Immediately cover with cold water. Let stand for about 3 minutes, or until cool enough to handle. Peel the eggs. Cut each in half, discarding the yolks. Chop the egg whites.
- Meanwhile, in a small bowl, stir together the mayonnaise, green onion, celery, bell pepper, mustard, turmeric, paprika, and pepper. Put aside.
- Gently stir the egg whites into the mayonnaise mixture.
- Line each pita half with 6 spinach leaves. Spoon the egg salad into the pita halves.

8.16 No-Yolk Egg Salad Pita Sandwiches

Servings: 4 persons

Preparation time: 10 minutes

Cooking Time: 17 minutes

Nutritional information: (Per Serving): Calories 157, Total Fat 4.5 g, Carbohydrates 22 g, Protein 9 g

Ingredients:

- 6 large eggs
- ¼ cup light mayonnaise
- 1 medium green onion or ¼ medium shallot, finely chopped
- 1 medium rib of celery, finely chopped
- ½ medium red bell pepper, finely chopped
- 1 tablespoon yellow mustard (lowest sodium available)
- ¼ teaspoon ground turmeric
- ¼ to ½ teaspoon paprika
- ¼ teaspoon pepper
- 2 6-inch whole-grain pita pockets, halved
- 24 baby spinach leaves

Directions:

- Put the eggs in a single layer in a large saucepan. Cover with cold water by 1 inch. Bring to a rolling boil, covered, over high heat. Remove from the heat. Let stand, covered, for 15 minutes. Drain. Immediately cover with cold water. Let stand for about 3 minutes, or until cool enough to handle. Peel the eggs. Cut each in half, discarding the yolks. Chop the egg whites.
- Meanwhile, in a small bowl, stir together the mayonnaise, green onion, celery, bell pepper, mustard, turmeric, paprika, and pepper. Put aside.
- Gently stir the egg whites into the mayonnaise mixture.
- Line each pita half with 6 spinach leaves. Spoon the egg salad into the pita halves.

8.17 Cheddar and Vegetable Crustless Quiche

Servings: 6 persons

Preparation time: 12 minutes

Cooking Time: 40 to 45 minutes

Nutritional information: (Per Serving): Calories 119, Total Fat 4.0 g, Carbohydrates 10 g, Protein 11 g

Ingredients:

- Cooking spray
- 3 large eggs
- 3 large egg whites
- ½ cup fat-free milk
- 2 tablespoons all-purpose flour
- ¼ teaspoon dried thyme, crumbled
- 1/8 teaspoon salt
- 1/8 teaspoon pepper
- 1 cup shredded low-fat sharp Cheddar cheese
- 1 cup bottled roasted red bell peppers, drained, patted dry, and chopped
- ¾ cup frozen whole-kernel corn, thawed
- 2 medium green onions, thinly sliced

Directions:

- Heat the oven to 350°F. Lightly spray a 9-inch glass pie pan with cooking oil spray.
- In a large bowl, whisk the eggs, egg whites, milk, flour, thyme, salt, and pepper until smooth. Stir in the remaining ingredients. Pour into the pie pan.
- Bake for 40 to 45 minutes, or till the top of the quiche is golden, and the center is set (doesn't jiggle when the pan is lightly shaken). Let stand for 5 minutes before slicing.

8.18 Greek Omelet

Servings: 2 persons

Preparation time: 10 minutes

Cooking Time: 5 minutes

Nutritional information: (Per Serving): Calories 147, Total Fat 9.5 g, Carbohydrates 4 g, Protein 13 g

Ingredients:

- 2 large eggs
- 2 large egg whites
- 1 tablespoon finely chopped onion
- 1 tablespoon water
- ¼ teaspoon dried oregano, crumbled
- 1 teaspoon olive oil
- ½ cup shredded spinach
- ¼ cup chopped tomato
- 1 tablespoon finely chopped kalamata olives
- 1 tablespoon crumbled low-fat feta cheese
- 2 tablespoons fat-free plain Greek yogurt
- ¼ teaspoon pepper (coarsely ground preferred)

Directions:

- In a bowl, whisk the eggs, egg whites, onion, water, and oregano.
- In a large nonstick pan, heat the oil over medium heat, swirling to coat the bottom. Pour the egg mixture into the skillet, swirling to coat the bottom. Cook for 30 seconds. Using a spatula, carefully lift the cooked edge of the omelet and tilt the skillet, so the uncooked portion flows under the edge. Cook until no runniness remains, repeating the lift-and-tilt procedure once or twice at other places along the edge if needed.
- Sprinkle the spinach, tomato, olives, and feta over half of the omelet. Using a spatula, carefully fold the half with no filling over the other half.
- Gently slide the omelet onto a dinner plate. Cut the omelet in half. Transfer one half to another plate. Top each serving with 1 tablespoon of yogurt. Sprinkle with pepper.

8.19 Green Chile and Tortilla Casserole

Servings: 4 persons

Preparation time: 10 minutes

Cooking Time: 30 to 35 minutes

Nutritional information: (Per Serving): Calories 170, Total Fat 4.5 g, Carbohydrates 18 g, Protein 14 g

Ingredients:

- Cooking spray
- 6 6-inch corn tortillas, torn into bite-size pieces
- 1 4-ounce can chop green chiles, drained
- 1 cup shredded low-fat Cheddar cheese
- 1 medium red bell pepper, chopped
- 4 medium green onions, thinly sliced
- 1 cup low-fat buttermilk
- 1 large whole egg
- 2 large egg whites

Directions:

- Heat the oven to 325°F. Lightly spray a 9-inch square glass baking dish with cooking oil spray.
- In the order listed, layer half of each of the following ingredients in the baking dish: tortillas, green chiles, Cheddar, bell pepper, and green onions. Repeat. Put aside.

- In a small bowl, whisk the buttermilk, egg, and egg whites. Gently pour over the casserole.
- Bake for 30 to 35 minutes, or until a knife inserted near the center comes out clean.

8.20 Lettuce Bundles with Sweet Lime Soy Sauce

Servings: 4 persons

Preparation time: 15 minutes

Cooking Time: 5 minutes

Nutritional information: (Per Serving): Calories 162, Total Fat 4.5 g, Carbohydrates 23 g, Protein 9 g

Ingredients:

For Sauce

- 3 tablespoons of sugar
- 3 tablespoons fresh lime juice
- 1½ tablespoons soy sauce (lowest sodium available)
- 2 teaspoons cider vinegar
- 1/8 teaspoon crushed red pepper flakes (optional)

Foe Filling

- 1 teaspoon canola or corn oil
- 4 ounces soy crumbles (meatless ground crumbles; about 1 cup), thawed if frozen
- 1½ cups finely shredded cabbage
- 1 8-ounce can slice water chestnuts, drained and finely chopped
- ½ cup finely chopped carrot
- 1/3 cup snipped fresh cilantro
- ¼ cup frozen green peas, thawed
- ¼ cup toasted sliced almonds

Directions:

- In a small bowl, whisk the sauce ingredients until the sugar is dissolved. Put aside.
- In a large nonstick pan, heat the oil over medium heat. Cook the crumbles for 4 minutes, or until heated through and beginning to brown, stirring occasionally. Remove from the heat.
- Stir in the remaining filling ingredients. Don't reheat.
- Put the lettuce leaves on a flat surface. Spoon about 1/3 cup of filling into the center of each leaf. Top each with about 2 teaspoons of sauce. Tightly roll up the leaves, jelly-roll style.

8.21 Mushroom Goulash

Servings: 6 persons

Preparation time: 10 minutes

Cooking Time: 25 minutes

Nutritional information: (Per Serving): Calories 302, Total Fat 2.5 g, Carbohydrates 53 g, Protein 19 g

Ingredients:

- 1 teaspoon olive oil
- ½ cup chopped onion
- ounces pre-sliced button mushrooms (about 2½ cups)
- 1 tablespoon sweet paprika
- 1 14.5-ounce can no-salt-add diced tomatoes, undrained
- ounces soy crumbles (meatless ground crumbles; about 2 cups), thawed if frozen
- ½ teaspoon salt
- ½ teaspoon pepper
- 12 ounces dried whole-grain no-yolk noodles
- ½ cup fat-free plain yogurt
- 2 teaspoons all-purpose flour
- 2 tablespoons snipped fresh parsley

Directions:

- Warm the oil in a large nonstick skillet over medium-high heat, stirring to coat the bottom. Cook for 3 minutes, or until the onions are tender, stirring regularly.
- Add the mushrooms and mix well. Cook, stirring regularly, for 5 minutes, or until gently browned.
- Add the paprika and mix well. Cook, stirring regularly, for 1 minute.
- Combine the tomatoes, liquid, soy crumbles, salt, and pepper in a mixing bowl. Still, over medium-high heat, bring to a boil. Reduce the heat to low and cover for 5 minutes. Increase the heat to medium-high and bring to a moderate boil, stirring occasionally. Boil for 5 minutes on low heat.
- Meanwhile, cook the noodles according to the package instructions, but leave the salt. Drain well in a colander.
- In a small mixing dish, combine the yogurt and flour. Stir in the yogurt mixture once the tomato mixture has been gently cooked. Cook for 1 minute, stirring regularly, over medium-high heat. Serve the sauce on top of the noodles. Garnish with parsley.

8.22 Apricot-Teriyaki Tofu Stir-Fry

Servings: 4 persons

Preparation time: 12 minutes

Cooking Time: 14 minutes

Nutritional information: (Per Serving): Calories 263, Total Fat 10.0 g, Carbohydrates 36 g, Protein 8 g

Ingredients:

- 3 tablespoons all-fruit apricot spread
- 3 tablespoons teriyaki sauce (lowest sodium available)
- 2-3 tablespoons of vinegar (preferably balsamic)
- 1/8 teaspoon red pepper flakes (minced)
- ounces frozen cooked brown rice (about 2 cups)
- 1 tablespoon toasted sesame oil
- 1 medium red bell pepper, cut into thin strips
- 1 medium onion, cut into ½-inch wedges
- 6 ounces asparagus spears, trimmed and cut diagonally into 2-inch pieces
- 4 ounces light firm tofu, drained, patted dry, and cut into ½-inch cubes
- ½ cup sliced or slivered almonds (about 2 ounces), dry-roasted

Directions:

- In a small bowl, whisk the apricot spread, teriyaki sauce, vinegar, and red pepper flakes. Put aside.
- Prepare the rice using the package directions. Put aside.
- Meanwhile, in a large nonstick pan, heat the oil over medium-high heat, swirling to coat the bottom. Cook the bell pepper and onion for 2 minutes, stirring frequently.
- Stir in the asparagus and tofu. Cook for 2 minutes, or till the asparagus is tender-crisp. Stir in the almonds.
- Spoon the brown rice onto a platter. Top with the tofu mixture. Put aside.
- In the same skillet, bring the apricot spread mixture to a boil over medium-high heat, scraping the bottom and side of the skillet to dislodge any browned bits and stirring constantly. Drizzle over the tofu mixture.

8.23 Tofu Parmesan

Servings: 4 persons

Preparation time: 12 minutes

Cooking Time: 18 minutes

Nutritional information: (Per Serving): Calories 169, Total Fat 7.0 g, Carbohydrates 13 g, Proteins 13g

Ingredients:

- 1 teaspoon olive oil

- ¼ cup diced onion
- ½ teaspoon bottled minced garlic or 1 medium garlic clove, minced
- 1 14.5-ounce can no-salt-added diced tomatoes, undrained
- ¼ teaspoon dried basil, crumbled
- 1/8 teaspoon salt
- 1 large egg white
- 2 tablespoons water
- ½ cup plain panko (Japanese breadcrumbs)
- ¼ cup shredded or grated Parmesan cheese
- ½ teaspoon dried oregano, crumbled
- 1/8 teaspoon pepper
- 12 ounces light firm tofu, well-drained, cut into 8 slices
- 1 teaspoon olive oil and 1 teaspoon olive oil, divided use
- ¼ cup grated low-fat mozzarella cheese

Directions:

- In a skillet, heat 1 teaspoon oil over medium-high heat, swirling to coat the bottom. Brown the onions for 2 minutes, or until almost soft, stirring frequently.
- Stir in the garlic. Cook for 1 minute, stirring constantly.
- Stir in the tomatoes with liquid, basil, and salt. Using a potato masher, mash the tomatoes to make the sauce almost smooth. Bring to a boil, still over medium-high heat. Reduce the heat and simmer for 10 minutes or till the sauce is thickened. Cover to keep warm. Put aside.
- Meanwhile, in a small shallow dish, whisk together the egg white and water.
- In a shallow dish, stir together the panko, Parmesan, oregano, and pepper.
- Put the dishes and a large plate in a row, assembly-line fashion. Dip 1 slice of tofu in the egg white mixture, turning to coat and letting any excess drip off. Dip in the panko mixture, turning to coat. Using your fingertips, gently press the panko mixture, so it adheres to the tofu. Transfer to the plate. Repeat with the remaining tofu.
- In a large nonstick pan, heat 1 teaspoon oil over medium heat, swirling to coat the bottom. Cook half the tofu for 2 to 3 minutes on each side, or till the coating is well browned. Transfer to a separate large plate. Cover to keep warm. Repeat with the final 1 teaspoon oil and remaining tofu.
- Arrange the tofu on plates. Top with the sauce. Sprinkle with the mozzarella.

8.24 Sesame Tofu and Vegetable Stir-Fry

Servings: 4 persons

Preparation time: 15 minutes

Cooking Time: 10 minutes

Nutritional information: (Per Serving): Calories 183, Total Fat 5.0 g, Carbohydrates 24 g, Protein 11 g

Ingredients:

- 2 tablespoons fresh lime juice
- 2 tablespoons soy sauce (lowest sodium available)
- 1 teaspoon cornstarch
- 1/8 teaspoon crushed red pepper flakes
- ounces frozen cooked brown rice (about 2 cups)
- 2 teaspoons toasted sesame oil
- 2 teaspoons minced peeled gingerroot
- 1 teaspoon bottled minced garlic or 2 medium garlic cloves, minced
- 1 medium yellow bell pepper, cut into ¼-inch strips
- 2 medium green onions, cut into 1-inch pieces
- 12 ounces light firm tofu, well-drained, patted dry, and cut into ½-inch cubes
- 6 ounces baby spinach (about 6 cups)
- 1 teaspoon sesame seeds

Directions:

- In a small bowl, whisk the lime juice, soy

sauce, cornstarch, and red pepper flakes until the cornstarch is dissolved. Put aside.
- Prepare the rice using the package directions. Put aside.
- Meanwhile, in a large nonstick pan, heat the oil over medium-high heat, swirling to coat the bottom. Cook the gingerroot and garlic for 30 seconds, or until fragrant, stirring constantly.
- Stir in the bell pepper and green onions. Cook for 2 to 3 minutes, or until tender-crisp, stirring constantly.
- Stir in the tofu. Cook for 2 minutes, or until heated through, stirring frequently.
- Stir in the lime juice mixture. Add half the spinach. Cook for 2 to 3 minutes, or until just wilted, stirring constantly. Repeat with the remaining spinach.
- Spoon the rice onto a platter. Top with the tofu mixture. Sprinkle with the sesame seeds just before serving.

8.25 Tempeh with Asian Slaw

Servings: 4 persons

Preparation time: 10 minutes

Cooking Time: 18 minutes

Nutritional information: (Per Serving): Calories 214, Total Fat 8.0 g, Carbohydrates 19 g, Protein 20 g

Ingredients:
- 1 teaspoon toasted sesame oil
- ½ teaspoon bottled minced garlic or 1 medium garlic clove, minced
- 1/3 cup fresh orange juice (plus 1 to 2 tablespoons fresh orange juice or water as needed)
- ¼ cup plain rice vinegar
- 2 teaspoons soy sauce (lowest sodium available)
- ½ teaspoon ground ginger
- 12 ounces tempeh
- ounces broccoli slaw mix (about 4 cups)
- ¼ cup sliced green onions

Directions:
- In a large nonstick pan, heat the oil over medium heat, swirling to coat the bottom. Cook the garlic for 2 minutes, stirring frequently.
- Stir in 1/3 cup orange juice, vinegar, soy sauce, and ginger. Bring to a simmer, still over medium heat. Add the tempeh. Simmer, covered, for 10 minutes, turning once halfway through. Transfer the tempeh to a medium plate. Put aside.
- If the tempeh absorbed most of the liquid, add the extra 1 to 2 tablespoons of orange juice to the skillet. Add the broccoli slaw, stirring to coat. Cook for 4 minutes, or till the slaw is slightly wilted, stirring occasionally.
- Meanwhile, cut the tempeh into thin strips.
- Spoon the slaw onto plates. Top with the tempeh. Sprinkle with green onions.

8.26 Summer Succotash with Creamy Polenta

Servings: 4 persons

Preparation time: 15 minutes

Cooking Time: 15 minutes

Nutritional information: (Per Serving): Calories 242, Total Fat 4.5 g, Carbohydrates 23 g, Protein 10 g

Ingredients:

For Succotash
- 2 teaspoons olive oil
- ½ cup chopped onion
- ½ cup chopped red bell pepper
- ½ teaspoon bottled minced garlic or 1 medium garlic clove, minced
- ounces frozen baby lima beans, thawed
- 1 cup frozen whole-kernel corn, thawed
- ½ cup low-sodium vegetable broth

- ¼ teaspoon salt
- 1/8 teaspoon pepper
- 2 medium Italian plum (Roma) tomatoes, chopped
- 3 tablespoons snipped fresh basil

For Polenta
- 2 cups low-sodium vegetable broth
- ½ cup yellow cornmeal
- ¼ cup shredded or grated Parmesan cheese
- 1/8 teaspoon pepper

Directions:
- In a large nonstick pan, heat the oil over medium-high heat, swirling to coat the bottom. Brown the onions and bell pepper for 3 minutes, or until soft, stirring frequently.
- Stir in the garlic. Cook for 1 minute, stirring frequently.
- Stir in the beans, corn, ½ cup broth, salt, and pepper. Bring to a boil, still over medium-high heat. Reduce the heat and simmer, covered, for 4 to 5 minutes, or till the beans and corn are tender-crisp, stirring occasionally.
- Stir in the tomatoes.
- Cook for 1 to 2 minutes, or until heated through. Remove from the heat. Stir in the basil.
- Meanwhile, for the polenta, bring 2 cups broth to a boil over medium-high heat. Slowly whisk the cornmeal into the broth, whisking constantly.
- Cook for 1 to 2 minutes, or till the polenta is very thick, stirring (not whisking) constantly. Remove from the heat.
- Stir in the Parmesan and pepper. Spoon into shallow bowls. Spoon the succotash over the polenta.

8.27 Bean-Filled Chiles Rellenos

Servings: 4 persons

Preparation time: 10 minutes

Cooking Time: 15 minutes

Nutritional information: (Per Serving)): Calories 276, Total Fat 3.0 g, Carbohydrates 47 g, Protein 18 g

Ingredients:
- 4–5 extra-large poblano peppers
- medium tomatoes
- 2 garlic cloves
- one large onion, sliced into ½ inch slices
- 3 jalapeños
- 2 tablespoons of olive oil

Directions:
- On a sheet pan, roast the poblano and ranchero sauce ingredients.
- After the chilies have been roasted, slice them vertically and load them with mozzarella (or vegan ricotta) & black bean mixture.
- Combine the rancheros sauce spices in a mixing bowl.
- In a baking dish, bake the stuffed bell peppers with the sauce.

Chapter 9 Vegetables and Side Dishes

A diet rich in variety and color is essential to maintaining a healthy weight. To acquire at least one meal from each of the following groups on most days, aim to include dark green leafy vegetables, yellow or orange fruits, veggies, red fruits and vegetables, legumes (beans and peas), and citrus fruits in your diet. To satisfy a sweet hunger, place several cleaned and ready-to-eat entire fruits in a dish or keep chopped colored fruits in a bowl in the fridge for later consumption. Cooking new meals that involve more veggies may be a good idea. Recipes for salads, stews, and stir-fries just are a few examples of how to include more nutritious veggies into your meals.

9.1 Roasted Asparagus and Mushrooms with Rosemary

Servings: 4 persons

Preparation time: 10 minutes

Cooking Time: 10 minutes

Nutritional information: (Per Serving): Calories 58, Total Fat 2.5 g, Carbohydrates 7 g, Protein 4 g

Ingredients:

- 1-pound fresh asparagus, trimmed
- 8 ounces shiitake or button mushrooms, stems discarded if shiitake
- 2 teaspoons olive oil
- ½ teaspoon finely snipped fresh rosemary or ¼ teaspoon dried, crushed
- ½ teaspoon garlic powder
- 1/8 teaspoon salt
- Pepper to taste

Directions:

- Heat the oven to 500°F.
- Place the asparagus and mushrooms in a large shallow dish. Drizzle with the oil. Sprinkle with rosemary, garlic powder, salt, and pepper. Turn the asparagus and mushrooms gently to coat. Arrange them in a single layer on a baking sheet.
- Roast for 10 minutes, or till the asparagus is tender-crisp.

9.2 Toasted Barley Pilaf

Servings: 4 persons

Preparation time: 6 minutes

Cooking Time: 32 minutes

Nutritional information: (Per Serving): Calories 183, Total Fat 0.5 g, Carbohydrates 39 g, Protein 6 g

Ingredients:

- 1 cup uncooked pearl barley
- 2 cups fat-free, low-sodium chicken broth
- ½ cup sliced celery
- ¼ teaspoon finely snipped fresh rosemary or 1/8 teaspoon dried, crushed
- 1/8 teaspoon salt
- 1/8 teaspoon pepper

Directions:

- In a large, heavy skillet, cook the barley over medium heat for 10 minutes, or until lightly toasted, stirring occasionally.
- Slowly stir in the broth. Stir in the remaining

ingredients. Increase the heat to high and bring it to a boil. Reduce the heat and simmer, covered, for 20 minutes, or till the liquid is absorbed.

9.3 Broccoli with Creamy Dijon Sauce

Servings: 4 persons

Preparation time: 10 minutes

Cooking Time: 3 minutes

Nutritional information: (Per Serving): Calories 4, Total Fat 0.5 g, Carbohydrates 7 g, Protein 3 g

Ingredients:

- ½ cup fat-free, low-sodium chicken broth (plus more as needed)
- ½ teaspoon dried thyme, crumbled
- 8 ounces broccoli florets (about 3 cups)
- 2 tablespoons fat-free sour cream
- 2 teaspoons all-purpose flour
- 2 teaspoons Dijon mustard (lowest sodium available)

Directions:

- In a saucepan, bring ½ cup broth and the thyme to a boil over high heat. Stir in the broccoli. Return to a boil.
- Reduce the heat and simmer, covered, for 5 minutes, or till the broccoli is tender-crisp. Using a slotted spoon, transfer the broccoli to a large plate, leaving the cooking liquid in the pan. Cover the broccoli to keep it warm. Put aside.
- Meanwhile, in a small bowl, whisk the sour cream, flour, and mustard. Whisk the mixture into the broth. Cook over medium heat for 3 minutes, whisking constantly. Don't let the sauce boil. If the sauce is too thick, whisk in more broth, 1 tablespoon at a time, until the desired consistency.
- Remove the pan from the heat.
- Add the broccoli to the sauce, stirring gently to coat

9.4 Red Potatoes with Creamy Dijon Sauce

Servings: 4 persons

Preparation time: 5 minutes

Cooking Time: 10 minutes

Nutritional information: (Per Serving): Calories 40, Total Fat 0.5 g, Carbohydrates 7 g, Protein 3 g

Ingredients:

- 1-pound small red potatoes,
- cut into bite-size pieces, for the broccoli
- ¼ teaspoon dried dill weed, crumbled,

Directions:

- Preheat the oven to 350°F and place a big heavy baking tray in the oven. Preheat oven to 400 ° degrees Fahrenheit. (Keep the baking tray in the oven while it warms up.)
- In a medium mixing basin, combine potato, 1 1/2 tablespoons olives, garlic, and thyme; toss to coat. Place the potato mixture on a baking sheet that has been warmed, and season with 1/2 tsp salt and ½ teaspoon black pepper. Bake for 30 minutes at 400 degrees F, or until golden and tender, turning after twenty minutes.
- In a separate bowl, mix the remaining 1 1/2 teaspoons olive oil, 1/4 teaspoon salt, 1/4 teaspoon pepper, lemon juice, shallots, Dijon mustard, and tarragon. Serve with the dressing drizzled over the potatoes.

9.5 Brussels Sprouts with Orange-Sesame Sauce

Servings: 4 persons

Preparation time: 3 minutes

Cooking Time: 10 minutes

Nutritional information: (Per Serving): Calories 38, Total Fat 1.0 g, Carbohydrates 7 g, Protein 3 g

Ingredients:

- 2 teaspoons water
- 2 teaspoons frozen orange juice concentrate
- 1 teaspoon light tub margarine
- ¼ teaspoon sesame seeds, dry-roasted if desired
- 1/8 teaspoon salt

Directions:
- Prepare the brussels sprouts using the package directions. Drain well in a colander. Transfer to a serving bowl.
- Meanwhile, in a 1-cup glass measuring cup, microwave the water, orange juice concentrate, margarine, sesame seeds, and salt on 100 percent power (high) for 30 seconds, or till the orange juice thaws and the margarine is melted. Stir. Put aside.
- When the brussels sprouts are done, pour the sauce over them, tossing them to coat.

9.6 Gingered Bulgur and Dried Apricots

Servings: 4 persons

Preparation time: 8 minutes

Cooking Time: 7 minutes

Nutritional information: (Per Serving): Calories 142, Total Fat 0.5 g, Carbohydrates 32 g, Protein 5 g

Ingredients:
- 2 cups water
- 1 cup instant, or fine-grain, bulgur
- ¼ cup chopped dried apricots or mixed dried fruit bits
- 1 tablespoon grated peeled gingerroot
- 1/8 teaspoon salt
- ¼ teaspoon ground cinnamon

Directions:
- In a saucepan, stir together all the ingredients. Bring to a boil over high heat. Reduce the heat and simmer, covered, for 5 minutes, or till the liquid is absorbed.

9.7 Cauliflower with Peanut Dipping Sauce

Servings: 4 persons

Preparation time: 10 minutes

Cooking Time: 9 minutes

Nutritional information: (Per Serving): Calories 55, Total Fat 2.5 g, Carbohydrates 8 g, Protein 3 g

Ingredients:
- ½ cup water
- 3 cups cauliflower florets
- 4½ tablespoons unsweetened apple juice
- 1 tablespoon creamy peanut butter (lowest sodium available)
- ½ teaspoon grated lime zest
- 1 teaspoon fresh lime juice
- ½ teaspoon bottled minced garlic or 1 medium garlic clove, minced
- ¼ teaspoon curry powder
- 1/8 teaspoon cornstarch
- Dash of cayenne

Directions:
- In a saucepan, bring the water to a boil over medium-high heat. Boil the cauliflower, covered, for 8 minutes, or until tender-crisp. Drain well in a colander.
- Meanwhile, in a small saucepan, stir together the remaining ingredients. Cook over high heat for 5 to 7 minutes, or till the desired consistency, stirring occasionally. Serve the cauliflower with the dipping sauce.

9.8 Colorful Lemon Couscous

Servings: 4 persons

Preparation time: 8 minutes

Cooking Time: 8 minutes

Nutritional information: (Per Serving): Calories 150, Total Fat 0.5 g, Carbohydrates 32 g, Protein 6 g

Ingredients:

- Cooking spray
- 1 small green bell pepper, chopped
- 1 small red or yellow bell pepper, chopped
- 1 teaspoon bottled minced garlic or 2 medium garlic cloves, minced
- 1 cup fat-free, low-sodium chicken broth
- 1/8 teaspoon salt
- 1 cup uncooked whole-wheat couscous
- 1 teaspoon finely grated lemon zest
- 1 tablespoon fresh lemon juice

Directions:

- Lightly spray a medium saucepan with cooking oil spray. Cook the bell peppers and garlic over high heat for 5 mins, or until tender, stirring frequently.
- Stir in the broth and salt. Increase the heat to high and bring it to a boil. Stir in the couscous, lemon zest, and lemon juice. Remove from the heat.
- Let stand, covered, for 5 minutes, or till the liquid is absorbed. Just before serving, fluff with a fork.

9.9 Green Bean Toss-Up

Servings: 4 persons

Preparation time: 5 minutes

Cooking Time: 5 minutes

Nutritional information: (Per Serving): Calories 62, Total Fat 4.0 g, Carbohydrates 7 g, Protein 2 g

Ingredients:

- 12 ounces green beans, trimmed
- 1 tablespoon Dijon mustard (lowest sodium available)
- 1 tablespoon olive oil (extra-virgin preferred)
- 2 teaspoons Louisiana hot sauce (lowest sodium available)
- 1 tablespoon snipped fresh parsley

Directions:

- In a saucepan, steam the beans for 4 to 7 minutes, or until tender-crisp. Drain well.
- Meanwhile, in a bowl, stir together the mustard, oil, and hot sauce. Add the beans, stirring to coat. Stir in the parsley.

9.10 Citrus Kale with Dried Cranberries

Servings: 4 persons

Preparation time: 7 minutes

Cooking Time: 23 minutes

Nutritional information: (Per Serving): Calories 75, Total Fat 1.5 g, Carbohydrates 15 g, Protein 2 g

Ingredients:

- 3 quarts water
- 8 ounces chopped kale; any large stems discarded (about 5 cups)
- 1 teaspoon olive oil
- ¼ cup sweetened dried cranberries
- 2 tablespoons balsamic vinegar
- 1 teaspoon bottled minced garlic or 2 medium garlic cloves, minced
- 1/8 teaspoon salt
- 2 tablespoons fresh orange juice
- 1 teaspoon grated orange zest

Directions:

- In a stockpot, bring the water to a boil, covered, over high heat. Cook the kale, uncovered, for 8 minutes, or until softened, stirring occasionally. Transfer to a colander. Immediately run under cold water for 1 to

2 minutes, or until cool. Using the back of a large spoon, gently press on the kale to remove the moisture.

- In a large skillet, heat the oil over medium-high heat, swirling to coat the bottom. Cook the kale, cranberries, vinegar, garlic, and salt for 2 to 3 minutes, or until heated through, stirring frequently. Remove from the heat.
- Stir in the orange juice and zest

9.11 German-Style Noodles

Servings: 4 persons

Preparation time: 10 to 12 minutes

Cooking Time: 15 to 18 minutes

Nutritional information: (Per Serving): Calories 115, Total Fat 0.5 g, Carbohydrates 23 g, Protein 4 g

Ingredients:

- 6 cups water
- 4 ounces dried medium no-yolk noodles (3 heaping cups)
- ½ cup sliced carrots
- 1 cup chopped cabbage
- ½ cup fat-free sour cream
- 2 medium green onions, sliced
- ½ teaspoon caraway seeds
- ¼ teaspoon salt
- 1/8 teaspoon pepper

Directions:

- In a large saucepan, bring the water to a boil, covered, over high heat. Stir in the noodles and carrots. Reduce the heat and boil gently, uncovered, for 5 minutes.
- Stir in the cabbage. Cook for 3 to 5 minutes, or till the noodles are tender. Drain the mixture well in a colander. Return to the pan.
- Stir in the remaining ingredients. Reduce the heat to low and cook for 1 to 2 minutes, or until heated through (don't let the mixture come to a boil).

9.12 Bow Tie Pasta with Spinach and Radicchio

Servings: 6 persons

Preparation time: 10 minutes

Cooking Time: 10 minutes

Nutritional information: (Per Serving): Calories 73, Total Fat 2.0 g, Carbohydrates 11 g, Protein 3 g

Ingredients:

- 2 cups dried whole-grain bow-tie pasta or medium-shell pasta
- 1 teaspoon olive oil
- ½ teaspoon bottled minced garlic or 1 medium garlic clove, minced
- 1 to 2 tablespoons balsamic vinegar
- 2 ounces spinach, torn into bite-size pieces (about 2 cups)
- 1 cup torn radicchio
- ¼ cup shredded or grated Parmesan cheese

Directions:

- Prepare the pasta using the package directions, omitting the salt. Drain well in a colander.
- Meanwhile, in a small skillet, heat the oil over medium heat, swirling to coat the bottom. Cook the garlic for 1 minute, or until tender, stirring occasionally.
- Stir in the vinegar. Remove from the heat.
- Put the spinach and radicchio in a large bowl. Add the pasta. Pour the garlic mixture over all, stirring to coat. Sprinkle with the Parmesan

9.13 Angel Hair Pasta with Red Pepper and Tomato Sauce

Servings: 4 persons

Preparation time: 5 minutes

Cooking Time: 10 minutes

Nutritional information: (Per Serving): Calories 120, Total Fat 1.0 g, Carbohydrates 24 g, Protein 5 g

Ingredients:

- 1 large red bell pepper, chopped
- 2/3 cup fat-free, low-sodium chicken broth
- 1/4 teaspoon salt
- 1/8 to 1/4 teaspoon pepper
- Dash of cayenne
- 1 tablespoon plus 1 teaspoon no-salt-added tomato paste

Directions:

- Prepare the pasta using the package directions, omitting the salt. Drain well in a colander. Transfer to a large bowl.
- Meanwhile, in a small saucepan, stir together the sauce ingredients except for the tomato paste. Bring to a boil over high heat. Reduce the heat and simmer, covered, for 5 minutes, or till the bell pepper is tender.
- Transfer the sauce to a food processor or blender. Add the tomato paste. Process until smooth. Pour over the pasta, stirring to coat.

9.14 Sesame Pasta and Vegetables

Servings: 4 persons

Preparation time: 5 minutes

Cooking Time: 20 minutes

Nutritional information: (Per Serving): Calories 155, Total Fat 3.0 g, Carbohydrates 28 g, Protein 5 g

Ingredients:

- 8 cups water
- 16 ounces frozen vegetables, any combination
- 4 ounces dried whole-grain fettuccine or linguine, broken into pieces
- 1 tablespoon light tub margarine
- 1 teaspoon sesame seeds, dry-roasted if desired
- 1/2 teaspoon toasted sesame oil
- 1/8 to 1/4 teaspoon crushed red pepper flakes

Directions:

- In a large saucepan, bring the water to a boil, covered, over high heat. Stir in the vegetables and pasta. Return to a boil. Reduce the heat and boil gently, uncovered, for 8 minutes, or till the pasta is tender and the vegetables are tender-crisp. Drain well in a colander. Pour into a serving bowl.
- Add the remaining ingredients, stirring to coat.

9.15 Sugar-Kissed Snow Peas and Carrots

Servings: 4 persons

Preparation time: 5 minutes

Cooking Time: 15 minutes

Nutritional information: (Per Serving): Calories 48, Total Fat 1.5 g, Carbohydrates 8 g, Protein 1 g

Ingredients:

- 1 cup water
- 8 ounces baby carrots
- 4 ounces snow peas, trimmed
- 1 tablespoon light tub margarine
- 1 teaspoon sugar

Directions:

- In a large saucepan, bring the water to a boil over high heat. Add the carrots. Return to a boil. Reduce the heat and simmer, covered, for 5 minutes.
- Stir in the snow peas. Increase the heat to high and return to a boil.
- Reduce the heat and simmer, covered, for 3 minutes, or till the carrots and snow peas are tender-crisp. Drain well in a colander.
- In the same pan, cook the margarine and sugar over medium heat until the margarine is melted, stirring once or twice. Stir in the vegetables. Cook for 2 minutes, or till the vegetables are glazed, occasionally stirring to coat

9.16 Fresh Herb Polenta

Servings: 6 persons

Preparation time: 7 minutes

Cooking Time: 8 minutes

Nutritional information: (Per Serving): Calories 69, Total Fat 1.0, Carbohydrates 13 g, Protein 3 g

Ingredients:

- 2 cups water and 2/3 cup water, divided use
- 2/3 cup finely ground yellow cornmeal
- 1/8 teaspoon salt
- ¼ cup shredded or grated Parmesan cheese
- 2 tablespoons snipped fresh basil or 1 teaspoon dried, crumbled
- 1 teaspoon snipped fresh thyme or ¼ teaspoon dried, crumbled
- Cooking spray (if baking)

Directions:

- In a saucepan, bring 2 cups of water to a boil over high heat.
- Meanwhile, in a large liquid measuring cup (to make pouring easy), stir together the cornmeal, salt, and remaining 2/3 cup of water. Very slowly, pour the mixture into the boiling water, stirring constantly. Return to a boil. Reduce the heat to low and cook for 5 minutes, or till the polenta is thick and pulls away from the side of the pan, stirring constantly. Stir in the Parmesan, basil, and thyme. To serve soft polenta, spoon onto plates.
- For firmer polenta, continue by lightly spraying a 9-inch pie pan with cooking oil spray. Pour the hot polenta into the pie pan. Cover and refrigerate for at least 1 hour or until firm (can be chilled overnight).
- About 40 minutes before serving, heat the oven to 350°F.
- Bake the polenta for 30 minutes or until heated through.

9.17 Crisp Skin-On Oven Fries

Servings: 4 persons

Preparation time: 8 minutes

Cooking Time: 20 minutes

Nutritional information: (Per Serving): Calories 127, Total Fat 0.0 g, Carbohydrates 29 g, Protein 4 g

Ingredients:

- Cooking spray
- ¼ teaspoon salt
- ¼ teaspoon paprika
- ¼ teaspoon garlic powder
- 1/8 teaspoon pepper
- 3 medium baking potatoes, each cut into 8 wedges

Directions:

- Heat the oven to 450°F. Lightly spray a large baking sheet with cooking oil spray.
- In a small bowl, stir together the salt, paprika, garlic powder, and pepper.
- Arrange the potatoes with the skin side down in a single layer on the baking sheet. Lightly spray the Potatoes with cooking oil spray. Sprinkle with the salt mixture.
- Bake for 20 minutes, or till the potatoes are tender and the skins are crisp.

9.18 Garlic Quinoa

Servings: 4 persons

Preparation time: 4 minutes

Cooking Time: 20 minutes

Nutritional information: (Per Serving): Calories 167, Total Fat 2.5 g, Carbohydrates 30 g, Protein 6 g

Ingredients:

- Cooking spray
- ½ cup chopped onion
- 2 teaspoons bottled minced garlic or 4 medium garlic cloves, minced
- 2 cups water

- 1 cup uncooked pre-rinsed quinoa
- ¼ teaspoon salt

Directions:

- Lightly spray a medium saucepan with cooking oil spray. Brown the onions and garlic over medium heat for 3 minutes, stirring frequently.
- Stir in the water, quinoa, and salt. Increase the heat to high and bring it to a boil. Reduce the heat and simmer, covered, for 15 minutes, or till the water is absorbed.

9.19 Brown Rice Pilaf with Mushrooms

Servings: 4 persons

Preparation time: 10 minutes

Cooking Time: 20 minutes

Nutritional information: (Per Serving): Calories 108, Total Fat 1.0 g, Carbohydrates 21 g, Protein 3 g

Ingredients:

- Cooking spray
- 8 ounces pre-sliced button mushrooms (about 2½ cups)
- 6 to 8 medium green onions, sliced
- 1 teaspoon bottled minced garlic or 2 medium garlic cloves, minced
- 1¼ cups water
- 1 teaspoon very low sodium beef bouillon granules
- ¼ teaspoon salt
- ¼ teaspoon dried thyme, crumbled
- 1½ cups uncooked instant brown rice
- ¼ cup snipped fresh parsley (optional

Directions:

- Lightly spray a medium saucepan with cooking oil spray. Cook the mushrooms, green onions, and garlic over high heat for 5 mins, or till the mushrooms are soft, stirring occasionally.
- Stir in the water, bouillon granules, salt, and thyme. Increase the heat to high and bring it to a boil. Stir in the rice. Return to a boil. Reduce the heat and simmer, covered, for 10 minutes, or till the rice is tender. Stir in the parsley.

9.20 Southwestern Rice

Servings: 4 persons

Preparation time: 5 minutes

Cooking Time: 55 minutes

Nutritional information: (Per Serving): Calories 169, Total Fat 1.5 g, Carbohydrates 35 g, Protein 5 g

Ingredients:

- 2½ cups fat-free, low-sodium chicken broth
- 1/8 teaspoon salt
- 1 cup uncooked brown aromatic rice, such as brown basmati or brown Texmati
- ½ teaspoon ground cumin
- 1 medium tomatillo or tomato, chopped
- 1 to 2 tablespoons snipped fresh cilantro
- ½ teaspoon grated lime zest
- 1 teaspoon fresh lime juice
- ½ teaspoon minced fresh jalapeño

Directions:

- In a saucepan, bring the broth and salt to a boil over high heat. Stir in the rice and cumin. Return to a boil. Reduce the heat and simmer, covered, for 45 to 50 minutes, or till the rice is tender and the liquid is absorbed.
- Stir in the remaining ingredients.

Chapter 10 Bread and Breakfast dishes

Especially whole meal bread is rich in carbohydrates, which helps to maintain our digestive systems in good condition while also helping to manage cholesterol in the body and keeping us feeling fuller for longer periods. Bread includes a broad variety of vitamins and minerals, including the B group vitamins riboflavin (B1) and niacin (B3), which are essential for the release of energy from food as well as the maintenance of healthy skin, eyes, and nails. It includes the vitamin Folic acid, which is essential for pregnant women because it may assist to prevent central nervous system abnormalities such as scleroderma Bifida from developing. Bread has just a few calories in each slice. A medium-sized slice of bread has 77 calories, a medium-sized slice of brown bread contains 72 calories, and a medium-sized piece of whole-meal bread contains 79 calories.

10.1 Easy Mexican Cornbread

Servings: 14 persons

Preparation time: 15 minutes

Cooking Time: 5 minutes

Nutritional information: (Per Serving): Calories 144, Total Fat 5.5 g, Carbohydrates 22 g, Protein 3 g

Ingredients:

- Cooking spray
- 1½ cups yellow cornmeal
- ½ cup whole-wheat flour
- ¼ cup sugar
- ½ teaspoon chili powder
- ½ teaspoon cayenne
- 1½ cups low-fat buttermilk
- 1 11-ounce can whole-kernel corn with red and green bell peppers, drained
- 1 small red bell pepper, finely chopped
- 1/3 cup canola or corn oil
- 2 large egg whites, lightly beaten with a fork

Directions:

- Heat the oven to 425°F. Lightly spray a 13 × 9 × 2-inch baking pan with cooking oil spray. Put aside.
- In a large bowl, stir together the cornmeal, flour, sugar, baking soda, chili powder, cumin, and cayenne.
- In a bowl, stir together the remaining ingredients. Add to the cornmeal mixture, stirring until well combined. Pour into the baking pan, lightly smoothing the top.
- Bake for 15 minutes, or until a wooden toothpick inserted near the center comes out clean, and the top is golden brown. Transfer to a cooling rack and let cool for 5 minutes before slicing.

10.2 Garden Herb Biscuits

Servings: 12 persons

Preparation time: 10 minutes

Cooking Time: 10 minutes

Nutritional information: (Per Serving): Calories 76, Total Fat 1.0 g, Carbohydrates 15 g, Protein 2 g

Ingredients:

- Cooking spray

- 1 cup reduced-fat baking and pancake mix and 2 tablespoons reduced-fat baking and pancake mix (lowest sodium available), divided use
- ¾ cup all-purpose flour
- 2 medium green onions, finely chopped
- 1 small carrot, grated
- ¼ teaspoon dried dillweed, crumbled
- ¾ cup fat-free milk

Directions:

- Heat the oven to 450°F. Lightly spray a baking sheet with cooking oil spray. Put aside.
- In a bowl, stir together 1 cup baking mix, the flour, green onions, carrot, and dillweed. Pour in the milk, stirring just until a soft dough forms. If the dough is sticky, gradually stir in enough of the remaining 2 tablespoons baking mix to make the dough easier to handle.
- Drop the dough by tablespoonfuls onto the baking sheet (you should have 12 biscuits).
- Bake for 8 to 10 minutes, or till the biscuits are lightly browned on top. Transfer the biscuits from the baking sheet to a cooling rack.

10.3 Bran Muffin Breakfast Trifle

Servings: 6 persons

Preparation time: 10 minutes

Cooking Time: 0 minutes

Nutritional information: (Per Serving): Calories 177, Total Fat 1.5 g, Carbohydrates 37 g, Protein 7 g

Ingredients:

- 3 bran muffins from Refrigerator Bran Muffins, coarsely crumbled (about 3 cups)
- 3½ cups assorted fruit and ½ cup assorted fruit, such as peeled kiwifruit, cantaloupe cubes, hulled strawberries, blueberries, blackberries, raspberries, and chopped mangoes, or any combination, divided use
- 2 cups fat-free vanilla or fruit-flavored yogurt

Directions:

- In a 2½-quart glass bowl, such as a trifle bowl or airtight container, layer as follows: half the muffin crumbs, 3½ cups fruit, the remaining muffin crumbs, the yogurt, and the remaining ½ cup fruit. Cover and refrigerate for at least 6 hours.

10.4 Refrigerator Bran Muffins

Servings: 15 persons

Preparation time: 15 minutes

Cooking Time: 20 minutes

Nutritional information: (Per Serving): Calories 108, Total Fat 2.0 g, Carbohydrates 20 g, Protein 3 g

Ingredients:

- Cooking spray (optional)
- 1 cup all-purpose flour
- ¾ cup unprocessed wheat bran
- ½ cup whole-wheat flour
- 2½ teaspoons baking powder
- 1 teaspoon ground cinnamon
- ¼ teaspoon salt
- 1 cup fat-free milk
- ½ cup egg substitute
- 1/3 cup firmly packed light brown sugar
- ¼ cup unsweetened applesauce
- 2 tablespoons canola or corn oil
- 1/3 cup raisins, chopped dates, or mixed dried fruit bits

Directions:

- If baking the muffins right after preparing the batter, heat the oven to 450°F. If baking all 15 muffins, lightly spray one 12-cup muffin pan and 3 cups of a second muffin pan with cooking oil spray or use paper bake cups.
- In a large bowl, stir together the all-purpose flour, wheat bran, whole-wheat flour, baking powder, cinnamon, and salt. Make a well in the center.

- In a bowl, stir together the milk, egg substitute, brown sugar, applesauce, and oil. Add to the well in the flour mixture, stirring until the batter is just moistened, but no flour is visible. Don't overmix; the batter should be thick and lumpy. Fold in the raisins. Use the batter immediately or transfer it to an airtight container and refrigerate for up to one week.
- Whether you are baking the muffins right away or refrigerating the batter, don't stir the batter again. Fill the desired number of muffin cups two-thirds full of batter. Fill the empty cups with water so the muffins bake evenly, and the pan doesn't warp.
- Bake for 15 to 18 minutes, or till the muffins are browned.

10.5 Apple-Spice Coffee Cake with Walnuts

Servings: 10 persons

Preparation time: 20 minutes

Cooking Time: 1 hour and 10 minutes

Nutritional information: (Per Serving): Calories 177, Total Fat 5.0 g, Carbohydrates 30 g, Protein 4 g

Ingredients:

- **Cooking spray**
- **1 teaspoon canola or corn oil and 2 tablespoons canola or corn oil, divided use**
- **1 medium Granny Smith apple, peeled and thinly sliced, and 1 medium Granny Smith apple, peeled and coarsely shredded, divided use**
- **¾ cup whole-wheat flour**
- **Half cup all-purpose flour**
- **Quarter cup sugar**
- **2 teaspoons ground ginger**
- **1 teaspoon of baking powder**
- **1 teaspoon ground cinnamon**
- **¼ teaspoon baking soda**
- **¼ teaspoon ground cloves**
- **1/8 teaspoon salt**
- **¾ cup low-fat buttermilk**
- **1/3 cup light or dark molasses**
- **1 large egg**
- **½ teaspoon of vanilla extract**
- **2 tablespoons properly chopped walnuts**

Directions:

- Heat the oven to 350°F. Lightly spray an 8-inch round cake pan with cooking oil spray. Put aside.
- In a large nonstick pan, heat 1 teaspoon oil over medium-high heat, swirling to coat the bottom. Cook the apple slices for 5 minutes, or until soft and lightly browned, gently stirring occasionally. Transfer to a small plate. Put aside.
- Meanwhile, in a large bowl, stir together the flour, sugar, ginger, baking powder, cinnamon, baking soda, cloves, and salt. Put aside.
- In a bowl, whisk the buttermilk, molasses, egg, vanilla, and remaining 2 tablespoons of oil. Stir this mixture and the shredded apple into the flour mixture until the batter is just moistened, but no flour is visible. Don't overmix. Pour into the pan, lightly smoothing the top.
- Arrange the apple slices in an overlapping circle in the center of the batter. Sprinkle the walnuts over the batter.
- Bake for 25 to 30 minutes, or until a wooden toothpick inserted in the center comes out clean. Transfer the pan to a cooling rack and let it cool for 10 minutes. Place a large plate over the pan and flip the coffee cake onto the plate. Remove the pan. Immediately flip the cake back onto the cooling rack (the apple side will face up). Let stand for about 1 hour, or until completely cool.

10.6 Confetti Scrambler

Servings: 4 persons

Preparation time: 5 minutes

Cooking Time: 4 minutes

Nutritional information: (Per Serving): Calories 72, Total Fat 2.0 g, Carbohydrates 3 g, Protein 10 g

Ingredients:

- 1 teaspoon olive oil
- 1½ cups egg substitute
- 2 medium green onions, finely chopped
- ¼ cup finely chopped tomatoes
- 2 tablespoons shredded or grated Parmesan cheese

Directions:

- In a large nonstick pan, heat the oil over medium heat, swirling to coat the bottom. Cook the egg substitute for 1 minute without stirring. Sprinkle with green onions and tomatoes. Stir gently. Cook for 1 minute without stirring, or till the desired doneness. Remove from the heat.
- Sprinkle with the Parmesan. Serve immediately for peak flavor.

10.7 Rise-and-Shine Cookies

Servings: 15 persons

Preparation time: 10 minutes

Cooking Time: 10 minutes

Nutritional information: (Per Serving): Calories 112, Total Fat 3.5 g, Carbohydrates 18 g, Protein 3 g

Ingredients:

- ½ cup all-purpose flour
- ¼ cup whole-wheat flour
- ½ teaspoon baking soda
- ¼ teaspoon salt
- ¼ teaspoon ground cinnamon
- 1/8 teaspoon ground nutmeg
- ½ cup firmly packed brown sugar
- ¼ cup egg substitute
- 3 tablespoons canola or corn oil
- 1¼ cups quick-cooking oatmeal or regular rolled oats
- ½ cup wheat germ

Directions:

- Heat the oven to 350°F.
- In a small bowl, stir together the flour, baking soda, salt, cinnamon, and nutmeg.
- In a large bowl, stir together the brown sugar, egg substitute, and oil. Stir in the flour mixture, oatmeal, and wheat germ.
- Drop the dough by tablespoons about 1 inch apart on the baking sheet. Using your hand or the bottom of a glass, flatten it slightly to a 2-inch diameter.
- Bake the cookies for 10 minutes or until light brown. Transfer to cooling racks. Serve or let cool completely and store in an airtight container at room temperature for up to one week or freeze in a resealable plastic freezer bag for up to three weeks.

10.8 Whole-Wheat Buttermilk Pancakes with Blueberry-Maple Syrup

Servings: 4 persons

Preparation time: 10 minutes

Cooking Time: 0 minutes

Nutritional information: (Per Serving) Calories 344, Total Fat 6.5 g, Carbohydrates 64 g, Protein 10 g

Ingredients:

For Pancakes

- 1 cup whole-wheat flour
- ½ cup all-purpose flour
- 2 tablespoons of sugar
- 2 teaspoons baking powder
- ¼ teaspoon baking soda
- 1/8 teaspoon salt
- 1¼ cups low-fat buttermilk

- 1 large egg
- 1 tablespoon canola or corn oil
- 1 teaspoon of vanilla extract

For Syrup

- ¼ cup maple syrup
- ¼ CUP BLUEBERRIES
- 1 cup blueberries

Directions:

- In a large bowl, stir together the flour, sugar, baking powder, baking soda, and salt.
- In a small bowl, whisk the remaining pancake ingredients. Pour into the flour mixture. Stir until the batter is just moistened, but no flour is visible. Don't overmix; the batter should be slightly lumpy.
- Preheat a nonstick griddle or large nonstick skillet over medium heat. Test the temperature by sprinkling a few drops of water on the grill. If the water evaporates quickly, the griddle is ready.
- Using a ¼-cup measure, pour the batter onto the griddle, spreading the batter into 3½-inch circles. (You may need to make two batches to get 8 pancakes.)
- Cook for 2 to 3 minutes, or till the tops are bubbly, and the edges are dry. Turn it over. Cook for 2 minutes, or till the bottoms are browned.
- Transfer to a warm plate and cover to keep warm. Repeat with any remaining batter.
- Meanwhile, in a small saucepan, bring the maple syrup and ¼ cup of blueberries to a boil over medium heat. Boil for 1 to 2 minutes, or until some of the blueberries pop.
- Pour the syrup over the pancakes. Sprinkle with the remaining 1 cup of blueberries.

10.9 Homemade Muesli

Servings: 9 persons

Preparation time: 5 minutes

Cooking Time: 5 minutes

Nutritional information: (Per Serving): Calories 173, Total Fat 3.0 g, Carbohydrates 33 g, Protein 6 g

Ingredients:

- 1 cup uncooked rolled oats or quick-cooking oatmeal
- 1 cup whole-grain flakes or bran cereal
- 1 cup sweetened dried cranberries or mixed dried fruit bits
- 1/3 cup slivered almonds, dry-roasted
- ¼ cup firmly packed light brown sugar
- ½ teaspoon ground cinnamon
- 3 cups fat-free milk, divided use

Directions:

- In a large bowl, stir together all the ingredients except the milk. Transfer to an airtight container.
- For each serving, put 1/3 cup of the oat mixture in a cereal bowl. Stir in 1/3 cup milk. Let stand for 5 minutes, so the oats soften.

10.10 Overnight Mixed-Grain Cereal

Servings: 14 persons

Preparation time: 3 minutes

Cooking Time: 10 minutes

Nutritional information: (Per Serving): Calories 207, Total Fat 1.5 g, Carbohydrates 44 g, Protein 6 g

Ingredients:

- 1 cup uncooked steel-cut oats
- 1 cup uncooked pearl barley
- 1 cupwheat berries
- 1 cup sweetened dried cranberries, dried blueberries, or chopped dates
- 2/3 cupmillet

Directions:

- In a large airtight container, stir together all the ingredients.
- For each serving, in a saucepan, stir together1/3cup cereal mixture and2/3cup water. Let stand, covered, at room temperature overnight.
- In the morning, bring the cereal mixture to a boil, uncovered, over high heat.
- Reduce the heat and simmer for 5 to 10 minutes, stirring occasionally.

10.11 Mandarin Breakfast Parfaits

Servings: 4 persons

Preparation time: 5 minutes

Cooking Time: 0 minutes

Nutritional information: (Per Serving): Calories 184, Total Fat 1.5 g, Carbohydrates 39 g, Protein 7 g

Ingredients:

- 2 11-ounce cans of mandarin oranges, packed in water or light syrup, drained
- ounces fat-free vanilla or fruit-flavored yogurt
- 2/3 cup low-fat granola without raisins

Directions:

- In parfait glasses, make a layer of half of each ingredient in the order listed. Repeat.

Chapter 11 Desserts

The need for sweets may arise, first and foremost, in persons who eat at random times as a consequence of a strong rush of adrenaline after a substantial meal. The abrupt "jump" in insulin results in a fast reduction in blood glucose levels, which stimulates the craving for sweets as a result. Another contributing factor is the removal of dietary items that include a high concentration of complex carbohydrates, such as whole-wheat bread, grits, oats, bran, brown rice, and whole-meal pasta, among others. Their inclusion on the menu helps us to feel content after a meal and to compensate for hypoglycemia after a meal. In addition, the desire to boost one's mood via the consumption of sugar might be a contributing element. Sweet foods promote the synthesis of the hormone known as the "happy hormone" in our bodies. Your behaviors play a significant part in this as well. The more often we go for after-dinner sweets, the more used our systems get to the sugar — which means we grab sugary snacks throughout the day. Unfortunately, consuming sweets regularly is detrimental to your health. Reaching for sweets regularly may lead to the development of excess weight gain and obesity. Eating treats that are high in sugar and fat, such as cakes with cream, chocolates with toffee, iced buns, pancakes with sweet toppings, pastries, and so on, is detrimental to one's health. Instead of typical sweets, choose fruit-based desserts, whole-wheat flour, milk, almonds, and chocolate, milkshakes, handmade smoothies and salad, homemade cakes made with whole-wheat bread, and other comparable healthy alternatives.

11.1 Easy Cherry-Cinnamon Crisp

Servings: 9 persons

Preparation time: 5 minutes

Cooking Time: 30 minutes

Nutritional information: (Per Serving): Calories 96, Total Fat 2.5 g, Carbohydrates 17 g, Protein 2 g

Ingredients:
- 2/3 cup uncooked rolled oats
- 1/3 cup all-purpose flour
- 1/4 cup firmly packed light brown sugar
- 1 teaspoon ground cinnamon
- 1/4 cup light tub margarine
- 1 14.5-ounce can tart red cherries packed in water, drained

Directions:
- Heat the oven to 375°F.
- In a bowl, stir together the oats, flour, brown sugar, and cinnamon. Cut in the margarine until the mixture is crumbly.
- Pour the cherries into an 8-inch square glass baking dish. Top with the oat mixture.
- Bake for 30 minutes or till the topping is light brown. Serve warm.

11.2 Chocolate-Banana Mini Cupcakes

Servings: 6 persons

Preparation time: 15 minutes

Cooking Time: 12 to 15 minutes

Nutritional information: (Per Serving): Calories 114, Total Fat 3.5 g, Carbohydrates 19 g, Protein 2 g

Ingredients:
- Cooking spray
- 1/4 cup whole-wheat flour
- 1/4 cup all-purpose flour
- 3 tablespoons of sugar

- ¼ teaspoon of baking powder
- 1/8 teaspoon baking soda
- Pinch of salt
- ¼ cup mashed ripe banana (about ½ large)
- ¼ cup low-fat buttermilk
- 1 tablespoon canola or corn oil
- ¼ teaspoon of vanilla extract
- 2 tablespoons mini chocolate chips or finely chopped semisweet chocolate
- 1 large egg white

Directions:

- Heat the oven to 450°F. Lightly spray a 12-cup mini muffin pan with cooking oil spray. Put aside.
- In a bowl, whisk the flour, sugar, baking powder, baking soda, and salt.
- In a small bowl, whisk the banana, buttermilk, oil, and vanilla. Stir into the flour mixture until the batter is just moistened, but no flour is visible. Don't overmix; the batter should be slightly lumpy. Stir in the chocolate chips.
- In a small mixing bowl, using an electric mixer at high speed, beat the egg white for 2 minutes or until stiff peaks form (the peaks don't fall when the beaters are lifted). Using a rubber scraper, fold half the egg white at a time into the batter.
- Spoon about 1 round tablespoonful of batter into each muffin cup.
- Bake for 10 to 12 minutes, or until a wooden toothpick inserted into the center of a cupcake comes out clean. Transfer the pan to a cooling rack and let cool for 5 minutes. Serve the cupcakes warm or at room temperature.

11.3 Cranberry-Studded Rice Pudding with Sweet Orange Sauce

Servings: 6 persons

Preparation time: 10 minutes

Cooking Time: 55 minutes

Nutritional information: (Per Serving): Calories 185, Total Fat 0.5 g, Carbohydrates 39 g, Protein 9 g

Ingredients:

For Pudding

- 10 ounces frozen cooked brown rice (about 2 cups)
- 2 cups fat-free half-and-half
- ½ cup egg substitute
- 1/3 cup sugar
- 1/3 cup sweetened dried cranberries
- 1 teaspoon ground cinnamon
- 1 teaspoon of vanilla extract

For Sauce (Optional)

- 2 tablespoons firmly packed dark brown sugar
- 2/3 cup fresh orange juice
- 2 teaspoons grated orange zest
- 1 tablespoon light tub margarine

Directions:

- Heat the oven to 350°F. Lightly spray an 11 × 7 × 2-inch glass baking dish with cooking oil spray. Put aside.
- Using the package directions, microwave the rice until warm. Transfer to a medium bowl. Stir in the remaining pudding ingredients. Pour into the baking dish.
- Bake for 45 minutes. Stir. Bake for 10 minutes or till the pudding has thickened (it won't be firm).
- Meanwhile, to make the sauce in a large saucepan, stir together the brown sugar and orange juice. Bring to a boil over high heat, stirring occasionally. Boil for 2 to 3 minutes, or till the mixture is reduced to ¼ cup, stirring occasionally. Remove from the heat.
- Whisk in the orange zest and margarine. Put aside to cool slightly until the pudding is done.
- Spoon the pudding into custard cups or small ramekins. To serve the pudding hot, spoon the sauce over it. At room temperature, let

the pudding stand for about 15 minutes, then spoon the sauce on top. To serve chilled, cover and refrigerate the pudding and sauce separately for 1 to 12 hours.

11.4 Balsamic Berries Brulé

Servings: 4 persons

Preparation time: 10 minutes

Cooking Time: 2 minutes

Nutritional information: (Per Serving): Calories 96, Total Fat 0.0 g, Carbohydrates 21 g, Protein 3 g

Ingredients:

- 1 teaspoon sugar
- 2 tablespoons balsamic vinegar
- 1 teaspoon chopped fresh mint
- 1/8 to 1/4 teaspoon pepper, or to taste
- 1/3 cup fat-free sour cream
- 1/3 cup fat-free plain yogurt
- 2 tablespoons firmly packed light brown sugar

Directions:

- Preheat the broiler.
- In a 9-inch pie pan, gently stir together the berries and sugar. Let stand for 5 minutes, so the flavors blend.
- Stir in the vinegar and mint. Sprinkle with pepper.
- In a small bowl, stir together the sour cream and yogurt. Spoon over the berry mixture. Sprinkle with brown sugar.
- Broil the berry mixture 4 to 6 inches from the heat for 1 to 2 minutes, or till the brown sugar melts. Serve immediately for peak texture and flavor.

11.5 Grilled Peaches with Almond Liqueur

Servings: 4 persons

Preparation time: 8 minutes

Cooking Time: 10 minutes

Nutritional information: (Per Serving): Calories 170, Total Fat 1.5 g, Carbohydrates 32 g, Protein 6 g

Ingredients:

- Cooking spray
- 2 teaspoons fresh lemon juice
- 1 teaspoon sugar
- 2 tablespoons almond-flavored liqueur
- 2 firm but ripe peaches, halved
- 2 cups fat-free vanilla frozen yogurt
- ½ teaspoon ground cinnamon
- 1 tablespoon plus 1 teaspoon slivered almonds, dry-roasted

Directions:

- Lightly spray the grill rack with cooking oil spray. Preheat the grill to medium-high.
- In a small bowl, stir together the lemon juice and sugar until the sugar is almost dissolved. Stir in the liqueur. Put aside.
- Lightly spray the cut side of the peaches with cooking oil spray. Place the peaches with the cut side up on the grill. Grill for 3 minutes. Turn it over. Grill for 2 to 3 minutes, or until heated through and slightly softened. Transfer the peaches with the cut side up to a small shallow baking dish.
- Spoon the lemon juice mixture over the

peaches. Let stand for 10 minutes, spooning the liquid over the peaches occasionally. Transfer the peaches with the cut side up to custard cups or small ramekins. Spoon any remaining liquid (there won't be much) into the peach cavities. Top with frozen yogurt, cinnamon, and almonds.

11.6 Minty Fruit Parfaits

Servings: 4 persons

Preparation time: 15 minutes

Cooking Time: 0 minutes

Nutritional information: (Per Serving): Calories 156, Total Fat 0.0 g, Carbohydrates 32 g, Protein 6 g

Ingredients:

- 8 ounces fat-free sour cream
- ¼ cup confectioners' sugar
- 1 tablespoon chopped fresh mint
- 2 cups assorted cut fresh fruit
- 6 ounces fat-free lemon yogurt, lightly beaten with a fork if thick
- 4 sprigs of fresh mint (optional)

Directions:

- In a small bowl, stir together the sour cream, confectioners' sugar, and chopped mint. Spoon half into custard cups or small ramekins. Arrange half the fruit on top. Repeat.
- Refrigerate for at least 15 minutes (30 if possible). Just before serving, drizzle the yogurt over the fruit. Garnish with mint sprigs.

11.7 Sherbet Parfaits

Servings: 4 persons

Preparation time: 8 minutes

Cooking Time: 0 minutes

Nutritional information: (Per Serving): Calories 164, Total Fat 0.0 g, Carbohydrates 39 g, Protein 1 g

Ingredients:

- 2 cups raspberries or blueberries
- 1 tablespoon sugar
- 1-pint frozen sherbet, any flavor

Directions:

- In a bowl, stir together the berries and sugar. Using a potato masher or fork, mash the berries slightly.
- Spoon half the berries into parfait glasses. Spoon half the sherbet over the berries. Repeat. Serve immediately or freeze until serving time. If frozen, let stand at room temperature for 10 minutes before serving.

11.8 Ice Cream with Fresh Strawberry Sauce

Servings: 4 persons

Preparation time: 10 minutes

Cooking Time: 0 minutes

Nutritional information: (Per Serving): Calories 137, Total Fat 0.0 g, Carbohydrates 31 g, Proteins 23 g

Ingredients:

- 1 cup strawberries, hulled
- 1 tablespoon sugar
- 1 tablespoon orange-flavoured liqueur or fresh orange juice
- 1-pint fat-free ice cream, such as vanilla

Directions:

- In a food processor or blender, process the strawberries, sugar, and liqueur until smooth.
- Scoop the ice cream into bowls. Spoon the sauce (hot, warm, or chilled) on top. To make the sauce in advance, pour it into a small airtight container and refrigerate until serving time.

11.9 Dried-Fruit Truffles

Servings: 12 persons

Preparation time: 10 minutes

Cooking Time: 0 minutes

Nutritional information: (Per Serving): Calories 56, Total Fat 0.0 g, Carbohydrates 14 g, Protein 1 g

Ingredients:

- 2 tablespoons unsweetened cocoa powder (dark preferred), sifted
- Cooking spray
- 1 cup dried pitted plums (orange essence preferred)
- ½ cup dried pitted dates

Directions:

- Spread the cocoa powder in a shallow dish. Put aside.
- Lightly spray the chopping blade of a food processor or blender with cooking oil spray. Process the dried plums and dates until finely chopped, scraping the side as necessary.
- Moistening your hands periodically with cold water to keep the mixture from sticking, shape it into 24 truffles, each about 1 inch in diameter. After you make a truffle, transfer it to the dish. Turn the truffles to coat with cocoa powder. Transfer to a large piece of wax paper. Serve at room temperature. Refrigerate any leftover truffles in an airtight container for up to two weeks.

Chapter 12 4 Week Meal Plan

Day	Breakfast	Lunch	Snack	Dinner
1	Easy Mexican Cornbread	Marinated Hoisin Chicken	Strawberry-Spinach Salad with Champagne Dressing	Molasses-Marinated Tenderloin
2	Garden Herb Biscuits	Baked Chicken with Winter Vegetables	Mushroom Poppers	Spicy Penne with Greens and Beans
3	Bran Muffin Breakfast Trifle	Grilled Chicken with Strawberry-Fig Sauce	Mustard-Marinated Vegetable Salad	Flank Steak with Blueberry-Pomegranate Sauce
4	Refrigerator Bran Muffins	Cheesy Oven-Fried Chicken	Mushroom Quesadillas	Rotini with Creamy Basil-Edamame Sauce
5	Apple-Spice Coffee Cake with Walnuts	Chicken with Leeks and Tomatoes	No-Chop Cajun Coleslaw	Grilled Sirloin Steak with Lemony Horseradish Sauce
6	Confetti Scrambler	Chicken-and-Clementine Kebabs with Peach Glaze	Savory Snack Mix	Peanut Pasta and Vegetables
7	Rise-and-Shine Cookies	Baked Chicken with Crunchy Basil-Parmesan Pesto	Grilled Pineapple with Zesty Blueberry Topping	Sliced Sirloin with Leek Sauce
8	Whole-Wheat Buttermilk Pancakes with Blueberry-Maple Syrup	Skillet Chicken with Dried Berries	Homemade Corn Tortilla Chips	Tangy Yogurt-Tomato Fusilli
9	Homemade Muesli	Lemony Chicken with Tarragon Oil	Fresh Herb Potato Salad	Beef Fajitas in Lettuce Wraps

10	Overnight Mixed-Grain Cereal	Spicy Peanut Chicken	Banana-Kiwi Smoothies	Creamy Green Rice and Black Beans
11	Mandarin Breakfast Parfaits	Barbecue-Simmered Chicken Chunks	Tabbouleh	Easy Oven Beef Stew
12	Easy Mexican Cornbread	Baked Dijon Chicken	Purple Slurp	White-Bean Veggie Burgers with Avocado Topping
13	Garden Herb Biscuits	Poultry and Mango Stir-Fry	Tuna Salad Bundles with Lemon and Dill	Espresso Minute Steaks
14	Bran Muffin Breakfast Trifle	Quick Cassoulet	Fruit Kebabs with Honey-Yogurt Dip	Meatless Tamale Pie
15	Refrigerator Bran Muffins	Cornmeal Chicken Muffinwiches	Puréed Broccoli Soup with Lemon-Infused Oil	Healthy Joes with Pasta
16	Apple-Spice Coffee Cake with Walnuts	Turkey Tenderloin with Cranberry-Jalapeño Sauce	Warm Chicken and Papaya Salad	Vegetarian Couscous Paella
17	Confetti Scrambler	Southwestern Turkey Stew	Mushroom-Asparagus Chowder	Three-Pepper Pork
18	Rise-and-Shine Cookies	Velvet Turkey and Herbs	Melon-Chicken Salad	Lentils with Green Beans, Carrots, and Dried Currants
19	Whole-Wheat Buttermilk Pancakes with Blueberry-Maple Syrup	Salmon and Brown Rice Bake	Peppery Pumpkin Soup	Pork Roast with Horseradish and Herbs
20	Homemade Muesli	Spicy Sole and Tomatoes	Speedy Taco Salad	Quinoa-Vegetable Patties
21	Overnight Mixed-Grain Cereal	Tex-Mex Tilapia Packets	Beef and Vegetable Soup with Cilantro and Lime	Sesame Pork Tenderloin

22	Mandarin Breakfast Parfaits	Smoky Trout with Citrus Topping	Pork and Water Chestnut Salad with Curry Dressing	No-Yolk Egg Salad Pita Sandwiches
23	Refrigerator Bran Muffins	Pan-Seared Tuna with Mandarin Orange Pico de Gallo	Thirty-Minute Minestrone	Curried Lamb Stroganoff
24	Apple-Spice Coffee Cake with Walnuts	Tuna-Topped Barley with Kalamata-Basil Tomatoes	Layered Two-Bean Salad with Cheddar Cheese	Cheddar and Vegetable Crustless Quiche
25	Confetti Scrambler	Lemon-Garlic Scallops	Layered Pesto Spread	Kiwi Veal
26	Rise-and-Shine Cookies	Speedy Shrimp and Pasta	Curried Shrimp Bisque	Lettuce Bundles with Sweet Lime Soy Sauce
27	Whole-Wheat Buttermilk Pancakes with Blueberry-Maple Syrup	Sherried Seafood Sauté	Spinach and Brown Rice Soup with Ginger	Rosemary Lamb Chops with Lemon Sauce
28	Homemade Muesli	Tuna with Ginger Bok Choy	Mediterranean Black Bean Salad	Mushroom Goulash

Conclusion

Cholesterol may be present in every single cell in your body. Cholesterol contributes 10 to 20 percent of the entire weight of your brain tissue. Cholesterol is essential for the synthesis of bile salts, which are necessary for the emulsification of lipids in the intestines. Cholesterol is necessary for all of your cell membranes to maintain permeability and perform effectively. Finally, cholesterol is needed in the creation of vitamin D.

A high in carbohydrates, especially simple carbs, may result in increased triglyceride levels. High triglyceride levels are generally related to high cholesterol levels in general, as well as an increased risk of developing heart disease. Your daily habits have a big influence on your overall well-being. Eating a heart-healthy diet, as indicated in this book, participating in regular physical activity, maintaining a healthy weight for your height, abstaining from smoking, and refraining from excessive alcohol consumption are the key parts of a healthy bodybuilding lifestyle.

Being aware of how your health increases your risk of having heart disease and stroke is an essential component of taking appropriate care of oneself. Collaborate with your healthcare practitioner to learn about the characteristics that elevate your unique risk. Some variables, such as advancing age and family history, are inescapable, but many others may be controlled. For example, you may decide to give up smoking if you wish to. If you need to reduce weight, you may establish a strategy to accomplish so. In addition to physical diseases such as high blood pressure and high cholesterol, dietary adjustments, exercise, and medication, if required, may be used to treat or decrease them. Diabetes is one example of such a disease.

Maintain track of your own food choices in a similar journal to keep track of your daily eating habits and make a note of what you need to pay attention to over the next few days to stay on top of your game in the meanwhile. For example, you can see in the sample meal record that the doughnut more than doubles the total amount of fat consumed while also increasing the amount of potentially harmful saturated fat consumed. A little cookie as an alternative to an indulgent doughnut may allow you to save a significant number of calories and saturated fat in the process of satisfying your sweet tooth. Once you've kept a diary for a few days, you'll be able to see how the consequences of your actions have mounted up over time. With a little forethought and preparation, you may acquire control and balance over your whole eating regimen, whether it's via limiting your consumption of one kind of food or increasing your intake of a different type of food.

Printed in Great Britain
by Amazon